COLLECTED SONNETS

Books by EDNA ST. VINCENT MILLAY

POEMS

The Buck in the Snow
Second April
Renascence
A Few Figs from Thistles
The Harp-Weaver
Poems Selected for Young People
Fatal Interview
Wine from These Grapes
Conversation at Midnight
Huntsman, What Quarry?
Make Bright the Arrows
The Murder of Lidice
Collected Sonnets
Collected Lyrics
Mine the Harvest
Collected Poems
*Flowers of Evil, from the French
of Charles Baudelaire* with George Dillon

PLAYS

The King's Henchman
The Lamp and the Bell
Aria da Capo
Three Plays
The Princess Marries the Page

Letters of Edna St. Vincent Millay
edited by Allen Ross Macdougall

COLLECTED
SONNETS

of

Edna St. Vincent Millay

Revised and Expanded Edition

PERENNIAL LIBRARY

HARPER & ROW, PUBLISHERS   NEW YORK

Cambridge, Philadelphia, San Francisco, Washington

London, Mexico City, São Paulo, Singapore, Sydney

First PERENNIAL LIBRARY edition published 1988.

Designed by Ruth Bornschlegel

Library of Congress Cataloging-in-Publication Data
Millay, Edna St. Vincent, 1892–1950
   Collected sonnets: Edna St. Vincent Millay.
   1. Sonnets, American. I. Title.
PS3525.I495A6 1988   811'.52   83–48369
ISBN 0–06–055102–X   88 89 90 91 92 MPC 10 9 8 7 6 5 4 3 2 1
ISBN 0–06–091091–7 (pbk.)   88 89 90 91 92 MPC 10 9 8 7 6 5 4 3 2 1

CONTENTS

From *The Harp-Weaver*

From *The Buck in the Snow*

Fatal Interview

viii

From *Wine from These Grapes*

From *Huntsman, What Quarry?*

From *Wine from These Grapes*

EPITAPH FOR THE RACE OF MAN

PREFACE

In preparing this edition of Edna St. Vincent Millay's sonnets for publication, I turned to the files at Steepletop for a look at the poet's drafts of her foreword to the first edition (1941). The drafts are in pencil, the handwriting brisk. Fresh at once is the sense of Millay at work on the pages: revising here, refining there, until the piece takes shape. Throughout the pages in draft are musings on the sonnet and on sonneteers, which found no way into her final manuscript. Perhaps the poet never intended using them, perhaps they served as asides to herself in the process of working out what she had to say. Whatever their purpose, they are winsome, witty, and keen. For the enjoyment of the reader, I take the liberty of quoting one of them:

> I had read much of the poetry of Wordsworth, and learned by heart several of his shorter poems, including the *Ode on Intimations of Immortality* (which is not so very short, after all; to memorize this poem indicates a considerable amount of enthusiasm for it on the part of the young reader) before I dared read any of his sonnets. For I did not trust him. I loved the sonnet; it seemed to me a peculiarly, a magically beautiful form of poetry, whether done in the English or in the Italian style. And what might the swollen ankles of Peter Bell [*A Tale*] not perpetrate in the way of deformity, in the way of ludicrous, hilarious, uproarious awfulness, if permitted

even to start to swell within the rigid contours of the sonnet? Would the sonnet burst? Would a galantine of Peter Bell be the result?—I dared not face it.

Then, one day, I just happened to read *Westminster Bridge*, and it was so beautiful that I did not know until after I had finished it whether it was a sonnet or a chant royal. Then I read it for a second time. Then I read all of them, over and over. Some *were* funny. There was the Stuffed Owl, of course, and a few other incredible pieces of awkwardness and utter absence of any sensitive foreknowledge of the possible reaction of the reader. But the sonnet, like a sharp-tongued wife, pulled Wordsworth together, made him pull up his socks, told him to shut up, when he had finished what he had to say, et cet.—et cet.

Millay's foreword, as it appears in the first edition, is reprinted in this volume. All of the sonnets she selected from her works for inclusion in the original collection are contained in the present edition, with the addition of twenty from the posthumous volume *Mine the Harvest* (1954), edited by the poet's sister Norma Millay. Preliminary plans for that book had been underway at the time of Millay's death in October, 1950.

The arrangement of the contents of this edition follows the chronological order in which the sonnets were first published in Millay's books of poems, with one exception. The sonnet sequence "Epitaph for the Race of Man" (1934) is placed at the very end, following the group of sonnets from *Mine the Harvest*. Placing the sequence there seemed appropriate to me and is consistent with the first edition, where Millay chose to depart from strict chronological order and conclude the book with "Epitaph."

Finally, a word about Norma Millay and her introduction to the collection. Norma died in 1986. For thirty-six years she was literary executor of her sister Vincent's estate. She knew Millay's poetry intimately, and spoke it wonderfully—most often from memory. The year before her death, Norma had been working intermittently on the introduction, parts of which she read to me and to Holly Peppe, a friend and a Millay scholar. It was Holly who reminded me, when I became literary executor, that Norma's manuscript of the introduction must be somewhere in the Steepletop house. We searched—and we unearthed: drafts in bold black ink on yellow legal pads, myriad notes marked for insertion. Together, Holly and I set to work piecing together the text and incorporating the notes. In our edited version of the introduction, as printed in these pages, we have endeavored to remain true to Norma's writing style and to the spirit of her quick, delving mind.

ELIZABETH BARNETT

June, 1987

FOREWORD TO FIRST EDITION

I have omitted from this collection several pieces in sonnet form which were not designed to be read as separate sonnets, and which apart from their context would not be fully understood. From *Conversation at Midnight*—where the passages in sonnet form were written not as independent sonnets but as speeches in a play, dependent for clarity upon the matter preceding them—nothing is included here. For a similar reason I have omitted from *Huntsman, What Quarry?* the short sequence, "From a Town in a State of Siege"; and from *Make Bright the Arrows,* seven of the nine sonnets which conclude the volume.

Two sonnets, both previously published in magazine form, but neither of them, through oversight, hitherto published in any volume of my poems, are included here. The first of these, beginning with the line, "I do but ask that you be always fair," appears in this collection as the opening sonnet of the group from *A Few Figs from Thistles*; the second, beginning, "Not only love plus awful grief," is part of the *Huntsman, What Quarry?* group.

Some time ago, while looking through the pages of an old workbook, I came upon one poem which I remembered vividly: the first sonnet I ever wrote. This, although it was written as a practice-piece, an exercise in sonnet-composition, and not intended ever to be published, I am printing in this foreword, as an object of possible curiosity and interest to readers of my *Collected Sonnets.*

I was about fifteen, I think, when I wrote it,—not very young to be trying my hand at my first sonnet. (Somewhat young, perhaps, to be burning in my lonely grate packets of letters yellow with age!) Here it is:

Old Letters

I know not why I am so loath to lay
Your yellowed leaves along the glowing log,
Unburied dead, that cling about and clog—
With indisputable, insistent say
Of the stout past's all inefficient fray—
The striving present, rising like a fog
To rust the active me, that am a cog
In the great wheel of industry today.
Yet, somehow, in this visible farewell
To the crude symbols of a simpler creed,
I find a pain that had not parallel
When passed the faith itself,—we give small heed
To incorporeal truth, let slack or swell;
But truth made tangible, is truth indeed.

The word "indisputable," as used in line four of the above, is not, I fear, an elegant attempt to stress my syllables after the manner of Shelley, but, rather, a sturdy, whole-hearted mispronunciation.

The word "cog" at the end of line seven is not brought in just for the rhyme. This is the only part of my first sonnet which may be said to be "real," as distinct from "fanciful." That year for the first time, during the months of my summer-vacation from High School (where I had taken a course in typewriting and stenography) I had a job: I was a typist in a lawyer's office in Camden, Maine.

The phrase "let slack or swell," in the next to the last line, is not so strained and far-fetched a metaphor as it sounds: it refers to the gradual ebbing and the gradual flooding of the tide, — an expression natural enough to a girl who had lived all her life at the very tide-line of the sea.

E. ST.V.M.

Steepletop
August, 1941

INTRODUCTION

There are instances in this collection of sonnets where Millay veers from the customarily charted course of the sonnet form, with its fourteen lines of iambic pentameter. The most striking of these metrical maneuvers is her conscious lengthening of the final line in each of the seventeen sonnets in the sequence "Sonnets from an Ungrafted Tree." For example:

And the blue night stood flattened against the window, staring through. (SONNET IV)

* * *

She had kept that kettle boiling all night long, for company. (SONNET XIV)

* * *

"I don't know what you do exactly when a person dies." (SONNET XVI)

Millay speaks of the need for this extension in a letter to the actress Edith Wynne Matthison (Letter 50 in *Letters of Edna St. Vincent Millay*):

Tell Mr. Kennedy [her husband, playwright Charles Rann Kennedy], before he has time to remark the fact himself, that I know very well the sonnets of the incomplete sequence are not perfect sonnets, — I made the fourteenth line an alexandrine purposely, — somehow they had to be ended in that way. Remind him also, if he refuses to read them open-mindedly (Mr. Masefield told me that he does not like "Interim" *because he does not like blank* verse) that [George] Meredith made some rather nice poems of sixteen lines each which we permit to be called sonnets.

At other times, the poet shortens her lines intentionally, and with thought and purpose. Three of her most powerful sonnets (my favorites, perhaps) are written in iambic tetrameter. Millay titled them "Three Sonnets in Tetrameter." The lines in these sonnets read more quickly than standard pentameter lines. Shortened to four beats, they relay an increasingly urgent message. The opening quatrains of these sonnets read:

> See how these masses mill and swarm
> And troop and muster and assail:
> God!—We could keep this planet warm
> By friction, if the sun should fail.
>
> * * *
>
> His stalk the dark delphinium
> Unthorned into the tending hand
> Releases . . . yet that hour will come . . .
> And must, in such a spiny land.
>
> * * *
>
> No further from me than my hand
> Is China that I loved so well;
> Love does not help to understand
> The logic of the bursting shell.

Finally, two sonnets taken from Millay's last notebooks, which I included in *Mine the Harvest* (1954), consist of thirteen lines each. It was logical for me to place these sonnets on facing pages in *Collected Poems;* not only are they both the same length, but they both deal with grief. They were written during the last year of Millay's life after her husband had died, when she was alone at Steepletop.

Upon first reading one of the two sonnets, I sensed that there was a line missing:

Grief that is grief and properly so hight
Has lodging in the orphaned brain alone,
Whose nest is cold, whose wings are now his own
And thinly feathered for the perchless flight
Between the owl and ermine; overnight
His food is reason, fodder for the grown,
His range is north to famine, south to fright.
When Constant Care was manna to the beak,
And Love Triumphant downed the hovering breast,
Vainly the cuckoo's child might nudge and speak
In ugly whispers to the indignant nest:
How even a feathered heart had power to break,
And thud no more above their huddled rest.

Reading the sonnet again, I felt I knew which line had been omitted: the seventh, or penultimate line of the octave. This proved to be so, as it was with the other sonnet on the subject of grief:

Felicity of Grief!—even Death being kind,
Reminding us how much we dared to love!
There, once, the challenge lay,—like a light glove
Dropped as through carelessness—easy to find
Means and excuse for being somewhat blind
Just at that moment; and why bend above,
Take up, such certain anguish for the mind?
Ah, you who suffer now as I now do,
Seeing, of life's dimensions, not one left
Save Time—long days somehow to be lived through:

Think — of how great a thing were you bereft
That it should weigh so now! — and that you knew
Always, its awkward contours, and its heft.

In both of these poems, there is a deviation from the rhyme scheme of the Petrarchan sonnet's octave — *abba abba* is shortened to *abba aba*.

In my opinion, Millay had no time for the one line that might hamper the driving movement in each of these tragic poems. And I like to think that perhaps she might not have been aware of dropping a line, that the force behind the sonnets was too pressing, too immediate, for her to adhere to the normal grace of fourteen lines.

Whether the poet knew she was leaving out a line, I can only surmise (and that is always dangerous): she certainly made no blueprint for her poems in progress. It is my contention that Millay did not spend her inspired and productive hours counting lines, but instead let the nature and power of the subject matter determine variations in form. From the moment of tugging inspiration, she put her genius to work to build the proper edifice or hut for her child.

NORMA MILLAY

Steepletop, 1986

COLLECTED SONNETS

Υ

Thou art not lovelier than lilacs, — no,

Nor honeysuckle; thou art not more fair

Than small white single poppies, — I can bear

Thy beauty; though I bend before thee, though

From left to right, now knowing where to go,

I turn my troubled eyes, nor here nor there

Find any refuge from thee, yet I swear

So has it been with mist, — with moonlight so.

Like him who day by day unto his draught

Of delicate poison adds him one drop more

Till he may drink unharmed the death of ten,

Even so, inured to beauty, who have quaffed

Each hour more deeply than the hour before,

I drink — and live — what has destroyed some men.

Y

Time does not bring relief; you all have lied

Who told me time would ease me of my pain!

I miss him in the weeping of the rain;

I want him at the shrinking of the tide;

The old snows melt from every mountain-side,

And last year's leaves are smoke in every lane;

But last year's bitter loving must remain

Heaped on my heart, and my old thoughts abide.

There are a hundred places where I fear

To go, — so with his memory they brim.

And entering with relief some quiet place

Where never fell his foot or shone his face

I say, "There is no memory of him here!"

And so stand stricken, so remembering him.

Υ

Mindful of you the sodden earth in spring,
And all the flowers that in the springtime grow;
And dusty roads, and thistles, and the slow
Rising of the round moon; all throats that sing
The summer through, and each departing wing,
And all the nests that the bared branches show;
And all winds that in any weather blow,
And all the storms that the four seasons bring.
You go no more on your exultant feet
Up paths that only mist and morning knew;
Or watch the wind, or listen to the beat
Of a bird's wings too high in air to view, —
But you were something more than young and sweet
And fair, — and the long year remembers you.

Υ

Not in this chamber only at my birth—
When the long hours of that mysterious night
Were over, and the morning was in sight—
I cried, but in strange places, steppe and firth
I have not seen, through alien grief and mirth;
And never shall one room contain me quite
Who in so many rooms first saw the light,
Child of all mothers, native of the earth.
So is no warmth for me at any fire
Today, when the world's fire has burned so low;
I kneel, spending my breath in vain desire,
At that cold hearth which one time roared so strong:
And straighten back in weariness, and long
To gather up my little gods and go.

Υ

If I should learn, in some quite casual way,

That you were gone, not to return again—

Read from the back-page of a paper, say,

Held by a neighbor in a subway train,

How at the corner of this avenue

And such a street (so are the papers filled)

A hurrying man, who happened to be you,

At noon today had happened to be killed,

I should not cry aloud—I could not cry

Aloud, or wring my hands in such a place—

I should but watch the station lights rush by

With a more careful interest on my face;

Or raise my eyes and read with greater care

Where to store furs and how to treat the hair.

Bluebeard

This door you might not open, and you did;
So enter now, and see for what slight thing
You are betrayed. . . . Here is no treasure hid,
No cauldron, no clear crystal mirroring
The sought-for Truth, no heads of women slain
For greed like yours, no writhings of distress;
But only what you see. . . . Look yet again:
An empty room, cobwebbed and comfortless.
Yet this alone out of my life I kept
Unto myself, lest any know me quite;
And you did so profane me when you crept
Unto the threshold of this room tonight
That I must never more behold your face.
This now is yours. I seek another place.

Υ

I do but ask that you be always fair,
That I for ever may continue kind;
Knowing me what I am, you should not dare
To lapse from beauty ever, nor seek to bind
My alterable mood with lesser cords:
Weeping and such soft matters but invite
To further vagrancy, and bitter words
Chafe soon to irremediable flight.
Wherefore I pray you if you love me dearly
Less dear to hold me than your own bright charms,
Whence it may fall that until death or nearly
I shall not move to struggle from your arms;
Fade if you must; I would but bid you be
Like the sweet year, doing all things graciously.

Υ

Love, though for this you riddle me with darts,

And drag me at your chariot till I die, —

Oh, heavy prince! Oh, panderer of hearts! —

Yet hear me tell how in their throats they lie

Who shout you mighty: thick about my hair,

Day in, day out, your ominous arrows purr,

Who still am free, unto no querulous care

A fool, and in no temple worshiper!

I, that have bared me to your quiver's fire,

Lifted my face into its puny rain,

Do wreathe you Impotent to Evoke Desire

As you are Powerless to Elicit Pain!

(Now will the god, for blasphemy so brave,

Punish me, surely, with the shaft I crave!)

Y

I think I should have loved you presently,
And given in earnest words I flung in jest;
And lifted honest eyes for you to see,
And caught your hand against my cheek and breast;
And all my pretty follies flung aside
That won you to me, and beneath your gaze,
Naked of reticence and shorn of pride,
Spread like a chart my little wicked ways.
I, that had been to you, had you remained,
But one more waking from a recurrent dream,
Cherish no less the certain stakes I gained,
And walk your memory's halls, austere, supreme,
A ghost in marble of a girl you knew
Who would have loved you in a day or two.

Υ

Oh, think not I am faithful to a vow!

Faithless am I save to love's self alone.

Were you not lovely I would leave you now:

After the feet of beauty fly my own.

Were you not still my hunger's rarest food,

And water ever to my wildest thirst,

I would desert you—think not but I would!—

And seek another as I sought you first.

But you are mobile as the veering air,

And all your charms more changeful than the tide,

Wherefore to be inconstant is no care:

I have but to continue at your side.

So wanton, light and false, my love, are you,

I am most faithless when I most am true.

Y

I shall forget you presently, my dear,
So make the most of this, your little day,
Your little month, your little half a year,
Ere I forget, or die, or move away,
And we are done forever; by and by
I shall forget you, as I said, but now,
If you entreat me with your loveliest lie
I will protest you with my favourite vow.
I would indeed that love were longer-lived,
And oaths were not so brittle as they are,
But so it is, and nature has contrived
To struggle on without a break thus far, —
Whether or not we find what we are seeking
Is idle, biologically speaking.

Υ

We talk of taxes, and I call you friend;

Well, such you are,—but well enough we know

How thick about us root, how rankly grow

Those subtle weeds no man has need to tend,

That flourish through neglect, and soon must send

Perfume too sweet upon us and overthrow

Our steady senses; how such matters go

We are aware, and how such matters end.

Yet shall be told no meagre passion here;

With lovers such as we forevermore

Isolde drinks the draught, and Guinevere

Receives the Table's ruin through her door,

Francesca, with the loud surf at her ear,

Lets fall the coloured book upon the floor.

Υ

Into the golden vessel of great song
Let us pour all our passion; breast to breast
Let other lovers lie, in love and rest;
Not we,—articulate, so, but with the tongue
Of all the world: the churning blood, the long
Shuddering quiet, the desperate hot palms pressed
Sharply together upon the escaping guest,
The common soul, unguarded, and grown strong.
Longing alone is singer to the lute;
Let still on nettles in the open sigh
The minstrel, that in slumber is as mute
As any man, and love be far and high,
That else forsakes the topmost branch, a fruit
Found on the ground by every passer-by.

Υ

Not with libations, but with shouts and laughter
We drenched the altars of Love's sacred grove,
Shaking to earth green fruits, impatient after
The launching of the coloured moths of Love.
Love's proper myrtle and his mother's zone
We bound about our irreligious brows,
And fettered him with garlands of our own,
And spread a banquet in his frugal house.
Not yet the god has spoken; but I fear
Though we should break our bodies in his flame,
And pour our blood upon his altar, here
Henceforward is a grove without a name,
A pasture to the shaggy goats of Pan,
Whence flee forever a woman and a man.

Υ

Only until this cigarette is ended,

A little moment at the end of all,

While on the floor the quiet ashes fall,

And in the firelight to a lance extended,

Bizarrely with the jazzing music blended,

The broken shadow dances on the wall,

I will permit my memory to recall

The vision of you, by all my dreams attended.

And then adieu, — farewell! — the dream is done.

Yours is a face of which I can forget

The colour and the features, every one,

The words not ever, and the smiles not yet;

But in your day this moment is the sun

Upon a hill, after the sun has set.

Υ

Once more into my arid days like dew,
Like wind from an oasis, or the sound
Of cold sweet water bubbling underground,
A treacherous messenger, the thought of you
Comes to destroy me; once more I renew
Firm faith in your abundance, whom I found
Long since to be but just one other mound
Of sand, whereon no green thing ever grew.
And once again, and wiser in no wise,
I chase your coloured phantom on the air,
And sob and curse and fall and weep and rise
And stumble pitifully on to where,
Miserable and lost, with stinging eyes,
Once more I clasp, — and there is nothing there.

No rose that in a garden ever grew,

In Homer's or in Omar's or in mine,

Though buried under centuries of fine

Dead dust of roses, shut from sun and dew

Forever, and forever lost from view,

But must again in fragrance rich as wine

The gray aisles of the air incarnadine

When the old summers surge into a new.

Thus when I swear, "I love with all my heart,"

'Tis with the heart of Lilith that I swear,

'Tis with the love of Lesbia and Lucrece;

And thus as well my love must lose some part

Of what it is, had Helen been less fair,

Or perished young, or stayed at home in Greece.

Υ

When I too long have looked upon your face,
Wherein for me a brightness unobscured
Save by the mists of brightness has its place,
And terrible beauty not to be endured,
I turn away reluctant from your light,
And stand irresolute, a mind undone,
A silly, dazzled thing deprived of sight
From having looked too long upon the sun.
Then is my daily life a narrow room
In which a little while, uncertainly,
Surrounded by impenetrable gloom,
Among familiar things grown strange to me
Making my way, I pause, and feel, and hark,
Till I become accustomed to the dark.

Y

And you as well must die, belovèd dust,
And all your beauty stand you in no stead;
This flawless, vital hand, this perfect head,
This body of flame and steel, before the gust
Of Death, or under his autumnal frost,
Shall be as any leaf, be no less dead
Than the first leaf that fell, — this wonder fled,
Altered, estranged, disintegrated, lost.
Nor shall my love avail you in your hour.
In spite of all my love, you will arise
Upon that day and wander down the air
Obscurely as the unattended flower,
It mattering not how beautiful you were,
Or how belovèd above all else that dies.

Υ

Let you not say of me when I am old,

In pretty worship of my withered hands

Forgetting who I am, and how the sands

Of such a life as mine run red and gold

Even to the ultimate sifting dust, "Behold,

Here walketh passionless age!"—for there expands

A curious superstition in these lands,

And by its leave some weightless tales are told.

In me no lenten wicks watch out the night;

I am the booth where Folly holds her fair;

Impious no less in ruin than in strength,

When I lie crumbled to the earth at length,

Let you not say, "Upon this reverend site

The righteous groaned and beat their breasts in prayer."

Ⓨ

Oh, my belovèd, have you thought of this:
How in the years to come unscrupulous Time,
More cruel than Death, will tear you from my kiss,
And make you old, and leave me in my prime?
How you and I, who scale together yet
A little while the sweet, immortal height
No pilgrim may remember or forget,
As sure as the world turns, some granite night
Shall lie awake and know the gracious flame
Gone out forever on the mutual stone;
And call to mind that on the day you came
I was a child, and you a hero grown?—
And the night pass, and the strange morning break
Upon our anguish for each other's sake!

Y

As to some lovely temple, tenantless

Long since, that once was sweet with shivering brass,

Knowing well its altars ruined and the grass

Grown up between the stones, yet from excess

Of grief hard driven, or great loneliness,

The worshiper returns, and those who pass

Marvel him crying on a name that was, —

So is it now with me in my distress.

Your body was a temple to Delight;

Cold are its ashes whence the breath is fled;

Yet here one time your spirit was wont to move;

Here might I hope to find you day or night;

And here I come to look for you, my love,

Even now, foolishly, knowing you are dead.

Y

Cherish you then the hope I shall forget
At length, my lord, Pieria?—put away
For your so passing sake, this mouth of clay,
These mortal bones against my body set,
For all the puny fever and frail sweat
Of human love,—renounce for these, I say,
The Singing Mountain's memory, and betray
The silent lyre that hangs upon me yet?
Ah, but indeed, some day shall you awake,
Rather, from dreams of me, that at your side
So many nights, a lover and a bride,
But stern in my soul's chastity, have lain,
To walk the world forever for my sake,
And in each chamber find me gone again!

Ƴ

When you, that at this moment are to me
Dearer than words on paper, shall depart,
And be no more the warder of my heart,
Whereof again myself shall hold the key;
And be no more—what now you seem to be—
The sun, from which all excellences start
In a round nimbus, nor a broken dart
Of moonlight, even, splintered on the sea;
I shall remember only of this hour—
And weep somewhat, as now you see me weep—
The pathos of your love, that, like a flower,
Fearful of death yet amorous of sleep,
Droops for a moment and beholds, dismayed,
The wind whereon its petals shall be laid.

Υ

That Love at length should find me out and bring

This fierce and trivial brow unto the dust,

Is, after all, I must confess, but just;

There is a subtle beauty in this thing,

A wry perfection; wherefore now let sing

All voices how into my throat is thrust,

Unwelcome as Death's own, Love's bitter crust,

All criers proclaim it, and all steeples ring.

This being done, there let the matter rest.

What more remains is neither here nor there.

That you requite me not is plain to see;

Myself your slave herein have I confessed:

Thus far, indeed, the world may mock at me;

But if I suffer, it is my own affair.

Υ

Love is not blind. I see with single eye

Your ugliness and other women's grace.

I know the imperfection of your face,—

The eyes too wide apart, the brow too high

For beauty. Learned from earliest youth am I

In loveliness, and cannot so erase

Its letters from my mind, that I may trace

You faultless, I must love until I die.

More subtle is the sovereignty of love:

So am I caught that when I say, "Not fair,"

'Tis but as if I said, "Not here—not there—

Not risen—not writing letters." Well I know

What is this beauty men are babbling of;

I wonder only why they prize it so.

Υ

I know I am but summer to your heart,
And not the full four seasons of the year;
And you must welcome from another part
Such noble moods as are not mine, my dear.
No gracious weight of golden fruits to sell
Have I, nor any wise and wintry thing;
And I have loved you all too long and well
To carry still the high sweet breast of Spring.
Wherefore I say: O love, as summer goes,
I must be gone, steal forth with silent drums,
That you may hail anew the bird and rose
When I come back to you, as summer comes.
Else will you seek, at some not distant time,
Even your summer in another clime.

Υ

I pray you if you love me, bear my joy
A little while, or let me weep your tears;
I, too, have seen the quavering Fate destroy
Your destiny's bright spinning — the dull shears
Meeting not neatly, chewing at the thread, —
Nor can you well be less aware how fine,
How staunch as wire, and how unwarranted
Endures the golden fortune that is mine.
I pray you for this day at least, my dear,
Fare by my side, that journey in the sun;
Else must I turn me from the blossoming year
And walk in grief the way that you have gone
Let us go forth together to the spring:
Love must be this, if it be anything.

Υ

Pity me not because the light of day
At close of day no longer walks the sky;
Pity me not for beauties passed away
From field and thicket as the year goes by;
Pity me not the waning of the moon,
Nor that the ebbing tide goes out to sea,
Nor that a man's desire is hushed so soon,
And you no longer look with love on me.
This have I known always: Love is no more
Than the wide blossom which the wind assails,
Than the great tide that treads the shifting shore,
Strewing fresh wreckage gathered in the gales:
Pity me that the heart is slow to learn
What the swift mind beholds at every turn.

Υ

Sometimes when I am wearied suddenly
Of all the things that are the outward you,
And my gaze wanders ere your tale is through
To webs of my own weaving, or I see
Abstractedly your hands about your knee
And wonder why I love you as I do,
Then I recall, "Yet *Sorrow* thus he drew";
Then I consider, "*Pride* thus painted he."
Oh, friend, forget not, when you fain would note
In me a beauty that was never mine,
How first you knew me in a book I wrote,
How first you loved me for a written line:
So are we bound till broken is the throat
Of Song, and Art no more leads out the Nine.

Ⴘ

Oh, oh, you will be sorry for that word!

Give back my book and take my kiss instead.

Was it my enemy or my friend I heard,

"What a big book for such a little head!"

Come, I will show you now my newest hat,

And you may watch me purse my mouth and prink!

Oh, I shall love you still, and all of that.

I never again shall tell you what I think.

I shall be sweet and crafty, soft and sly;

You will not catch me reading any more:

I shall be called a wife to pattern by;

And some day when you knock and push the door,

Some sane day, not too bright and not too stormy,

I shall be gone, and you may whistle for me.

Υ

Here is a wound that never will heal, I know,
Being wrought not of a dearness and a death,
But of a love turned ashes and the breath
Gone out of beauty; never again will grow
The grass on that scarred acre, though I sow
Young seed there yearly and the sky bequeath
Its friendly weathers down, far underneath
Shall be such bitterness of an old woe.
That April should be shattered by a gust,
That August should be levelled by a rain,
I can endure, and that the lifted dust
Of man should settle to the earth again;
But that a dream can die, will be a thrust
Between my ribs forever of hot pain.

Ɣ

I shall go back again to the bleak shore
And build a little shanty on the sand,
In such a way that the extremest band
Of brittle seaweed will escape my door
But by a yard or two; and nevermore
Shall I return to take you by the hand;
I shall be gone to what I understand,
And happier than I ever was before.
The love that stood a moment in your eyes,
The words that lay a moment on your tongue,
Are one with all that in a moment dies,
A little under-said and over-sung.
But I shall find the sullen rocks and skies
Unchanged from what they were when I was young.

Υ

Say what you will, and scratch my heart to find
The roots of last year's roses in my breast;
I am as surely riper in my mind
As if the fruit stood in the stalls confessed.
Laugh at the unshed leaf, say what you will,
Call me in all things what I was before,
A flutterer in the wind, a woman still;
I tell you I am what I was and more.
My branches weigh me down, frost cleans the air,
My sky is black with small birds bearing south;
Say what you will, confuse me with fine care,
Put by my word as but an April truth —
Autumn is no less on me, that a rose
Hugs the brown bough and sighs before it goes.

Υ

What's this of death, from you who never will die?
Think you the wrist that fashioned you in clay,
The thumb that set the hollow just that way
In your full throat and lidded the long eye
So roundly from the forehead, will let lie
Broken, forgotten, under foot some day
Your unimpeachable body, and so slay
The work he most had been remembered by?
I tell you this: whatever of dust to dust
Goes down, whatever of ashes may return
To its essential self in its own season,
Loveliness such as yours will not be lost,
But, cast in bronze upon his very urn,
Make known him Master, and for what good reason.

Υ

I see so clearly now my similar years
Repeat each other, shod in rusty black,
Like one hack following another hack
In meaningless procession, dry of tears,
Driven empty, lest the noses sharp as shears
Of gutter-urchins at a hearse's back
Should sniff a man died friendless, and attack
With silly scorn his deaf triumphant ears;
I see so clearly how my life must run
One year behind another year until
At length these bones that leap into the sun
Are lowered into the gravel, and lie still,
I would at times the funeral were done
And I abandoned on the ultimate hill.

Υ

Your face is like a chamber where a king
Dies of his wounds, untended and alone,
Stifling with courteous gesture the crude moan
That speaks too loud of mortal perishing,
Rising on elbow in the dark to sing
Some rhyme now out of season but well known
In days when banners in his face were blown
And every woman had a rose to fling.
I know that through your eyes which look on me
Who stand regarding you with pitiful breath,
You see beyond the moment's pause, you see
The sunny sky, the skimming bird beneath,
And, fronting on your windows hopelessly,
Black in the noon, the broad estates of Death.

♈

The light comes back with Columbine; she brings
A touch of this, a little touch of that,
Coloured confetti, and a favour hat,
Patches, and powder, dolls that work by strings
And moons that work by switches, all the things
That please a sick man's fancy, and a flat
Spry convalescent kiss, and a small pat
Upon the pillow, — paper offerings.
The light goes out with her; the shadows sprawl.
Where she has left her fragrance like a shawl
I lie alone and pluck the counterpane,
Or on a dizzy elbow rise and hark —
And down like dominoes along the dark
Her little silly laughter spills again!

Υ

Lord Archer, Death, whom sent you in your stead?
What faltering prentice fumbled at your bow,
That now should wander with the insanguine dead
In whom forever the bright blood must flow?
Or is it rather that impairing Time
Renders yourself so random, or so dim?
Or are you sick of shadows and would climb
A while to light, a while detaining him?
For know, this was no mortal youth, to be
Of you confounded, but a heavenly guest,
Assuming earthly garb for love of me,
And hell's demure attire for love of jest:
Bringing me asphodel and a dark feather,
He will return, and we shall laugh together!

39

Υ

Loving you less than life, a little less
Than bitter-sweet upon a broken wall
Or brush-wood smoke in autumn, I confess
I cannot swear I love you not at all.
For there is that about you in this light—
A yellow darkness, sinister of rain—
Which sturdily recalls my stubborn sight
To dwell on you, and dwell on you again.
And I am made aware of many a week
I shall consume, remembering in what way
Your brown hair grows about your brow and cheek,
And what divine absurdities you say:
Till all the world, and I, and surely you,
Will know I love you, whether or not I do.

Υ

I, being born a woman and distressed
By all the needs and notions of my kind,
Am urged by your propinquity to find
Your person fair, and feel a certain zest
To bear your body's weight upon my breast:
So subtly is the fume of life designed,
To clarify the pulse and cloud the mind,
And leave me once again undone, possessed.
Think not for this, however, the poor treason
Of my stout blood against my staggering brain,
I shall remember you with love, or season
My scorn with pity, — let me make it plain:
I find this frenzy insufficient reason
For conversation when we meet again.

Υ

What lips my lips have kissed, and where, and why,
I have forgotten, and what arms have lain
Under my head till morning; but the rain
Is full of ghosts tonight, that tap and sigh
Upon the glass and listen for reply,
And in my heart there stirs a quiet pain
For unremembered lads that not again
Will turn to me at midnight with a cry.
Thus in the winter stands the lonely tree,
Nor knows what birds have vanished one by one,
Yet knows its boughs more silent than before:
I cannot say what loves have come and gone,
I only know that summer sang in me
A little while, that in me sings no more.

Ƴ

Still will I harvest beauty where it grows:
In coloured fungus and the spotted fog
Surprised on foods forgotten; in ditch and bog
Filmed brilliant with irregular rainbows
Of rust and oil, where half a city throws
Its empty tins; and in some spongy log
Whence headlong leaps the oozy emerald frog. . . .
And a black pupil in the green scum shows.

Her the inhabiter of divers places
Surmising at all doors, I push them all.
Oh, you that fearful of a creaking hinge
Turn back forevermore with craven faces,
I tell you Beauty bears an ultra fringe
Unguessed of you upon her gossamer shawl!

Y

How healthily their feet upon the floor
Strike down! These are no spirits, but a band
Of children, surely, leaping hand in hand
Into the air in groups of three and four,
Wearing their silken rags as if they wore
Leaves only and light grasses, or a strand
Of black elusive seaweed oozing sand,
And running hard as if along a shore.
I know how lost forever, and at length
How still these lovely tossing limbs shall lie,
And the bright laughter and the panting breath;
And yet, before such beauty and such strength,
Once more, as always when the dance is high,
I am rebuked that I believe in death.

Υ

Euclid alone has looked on Beauty bare.

Let all who prate of Beauty hold their peace,

And lay them prone upon the earth and cease

To ponder on themselves, the while they stare

At nothing, intricately drawn nowhere

In shapes of shifting lineage; let geese

Gabble and hiss, but heroes seek release

From dusty bondage into luminous air.

O blinding hour, O holy, terrible day,

When first the shaft into his vision shone

Of light anatomized! Euclid alone

Has looked on Beauty bare. Fortunate they

Who, though once only and then but far away,

Have heard her massive sandal set on stone.

Sonnets from an Ungrafted Tree

I

So she came back into his house again
And watched beside his bed until he died,
Loving him not at all. The winter rain
Splashed in the painted butter-tub outside,
Where once her red geraniums had stood,
Where still their rotted stalks were to be seen;
The thin log snapped; and she went out for wood,
Bareheaded, running the few steps between
The house and shed; there, from the sodden eaves
Blown back and forth on ragged ends of twine,
Saw the dejected creeping-jinny vine,
(And one, big-aproned, blithe, with stiff blue sleeves
Rolled to the shoulder that warm day in spring,
Who planted seeds, musing ahead to their far
    blossoming).

II

The last white sawdust on the floor was grown

Gray as the first, so long had he been ill;

The axe was nodding in the block; fresh-blown

And foreign came the rain across the sill,

But on the roof so steadily it drummed

She could not think a time it might not be—

In hazy summer, when the hot air hummed

With mowing, and locusts rising raspingly,

When that small bird with iridescent wings

And long incredible sudden silver tongue

Had just flashed (and yet maybe not!) among

The dwarf nasturtiums—when no sagging springs

Of shower were in the whole bright sky, somehow

Upon this roof the rain would drum as it was

  drumming now.

III

She filled her arms with wood, and set her chin

Forward, to hold the highest stick in place,

No less afraid than she had always been

Of spiders up her arms and on her face,

But too impatient for a careful search

Or a less heavy loading, from the heap

Selecting hastily small sticks of birch,

For their curled bark, that instantly will leap

Into a blaze, nor thinking to return

Some day, distracted, as of old, to find

Smooth, heavy, round, green logs with a wet, gray rind

Only, and knotty chunks that will not burn,

(That day when dust is on the wood-box floor,

And some old catalogue, and a brown, shriveled

    apple core).

The white bark writhed and sputtered like a fish

Upon the coals, exuding odorous smoke.

She knelt and blew, in a surging desolate wish

For comfort; and the sleeping ashes woke

And scattered to the hearth, but no thin fire

Broke suddenly, the wood was wet with rain.

Then, softly stepping forth from her desire,

(Being mindful of like passion hurled in vain

Upon a similar task, in other days)

She thrust her breath against the stubborn coal,

Bringing to bear upon its hilt the whole

Of her still body . . . there sprang a little blaze . . .

A pack of hounds, the flame swept up the flue!—

And the blue night stood flattened against the

    window, staring through.

A wagon stopped before the house; she heard
The heavy oilskins of the grocer's man
Slapping against his legs. Of a sudden whirred
Her heart like a frightened partridge, and she ran
And slid the bolt, leaving his entrance free;
Then in the cellar way till he was gone
Hid, breathless, praying that he might not see
The chair sway she had laid her hand upon
In passing. Sour and damp from that dark vault
Arose to her the well-remembered chill;
She saw the narrow wooden stairway still
Plunging into the earth, and the thin salt
Crusting the crocks; until she knew him far,
So stood, with listening eyes upon the empty
    doughnut jar.

Then cautiously she pushed the cellar door

And stepped into the kitchen — saw the track

Of muddy rubber boots across the floor,

The many paper parcels in a stack

Upon the dresser; with accustomed care

Removed the twine and put the wrappings by,

Folded, and the bags flat, that with an air

Of ease had been whipped open skillfully,

To the gape of children. Treacherously dear

And simple was the dull, familiar task.

And so it was she came at length to ask:

How came the soda there? The sugar here?

Then the dream broke. Silent, she brought the mop,

And forced the trade-slip on the nail that held his

    razor strop.

One way there was of muting in the mind

A little while the ever-clamorous care;

And there was rapture, of a decent kind,

In making mean and ugly objects fair:

Soft-sooted kettle-bottoms, that had been

Time after time set in above the fire,

Faucets, and candlesticks, corroded green,

To mine again from quarry; to attire

The shelves in paper petticoats, and tack

New oilcloth in the ringed-and-rotten's place,

Polish the stove till you could see your face,

And after nightfall rear an aching back

In a changed kitchen, bright as a new pin,

An advertisement, far too fine to cook a supper in.

VIII

She let them leave their jellies at the door

And go away, reluctant, down the walk.

She heard them talking as they passed before

The blind, but could not quite make out their talk

For noise in the room—the sudden heavy fall

And roll of a charred log, and the roused shower

Of snapping sparks; then sharply from the wall

The unforgivable crowing of the hour.

One instant set ajar, her quiet ear

Was stormed and forced by the full rout of day:

The rasp of a saw, the fussy cluck and bray

Of hens, the wheeze of a pump, she needs must hear;

She inescapably must endure to feel

Across her teeth the grinding of a backing wagon
    wheel.

IX

Not over-kind nor over-quick in study

Nor skilled in sports nor beautiful was he,

Who had come into her life when anybody

Would have been welcome, so in need was she.

They had become acquainted in this way:

He flashed a mirror in her eyes at school;

By which he was distinguished; from that day

They went about together, as a rule.

She told, in secret and with whispering,

How he had flashed a mirror in her eyes;

And as she told, it struck her with surprise

That this was not so wonderful a thing.

But what's the odds?—It's pretty nice to know

You've got a friend to keep you company everywhere
   you go.

X

She had forgotten how the August night
Was level as a lake beneath the moon,
In which she swam a little, losing sight
Of shore; and how the boy, who was at noon
Simple enough, not different from the rest,
Wore now a pleasant mystery as he went,
Which seemed to her an honest enough test
Whether she loved him, and she was content.
So loud, so loud the million crickets' choir . . .
So sweet the night, so long-drawn-out and late . . .
And if the man were not her spirit's mate,
Why was her body sluggish with desire?
Stark on the open field the moonlight fell,
But the oak tree's shadow was deep and black and
    secret as a well.

XI

It came into her mind, seeing how the snow

Was gone, and the brown grass exposed again,

And clothes-pins, and an apron—long ago,

In some white storm that sifted through the pane

And sent her forth reluctantly at last

To gather in, before the line gave way,

Garments, board-stiff, that galloped on the blast

Clashing like angel armies in a fray,

An apron long ago in such a night

Blown down and buried in the deepening drift,

To lie till April thawed it back to sight,

Forgotten, quaint and novel as a gift—

It struck her, as she pulled and pried and tore,

That here was spring, and the whole year to be lived
    through once more.

XII

Tenderly, in those times, as though she fed
An ailing child—with sturdy propping up
Of its small, feverish body in the bed,
And steadying of its hands about the cup—
She gave her husband of her body's strength,
Thinking of men, what helpless things they were,
Until he turned and fell asleep at length,
And stealthily stirred the night and spoke to her.
Familiar, at such moments, like a friend,
Whistled far off the long, mysterious train,
And she could see in her mind's vision plain
The magic World, where cities stood on end . . .
Remote from where she lay—and yet—between,
Save for something asleep beside her, only the
  window screen.

XIII

From the wan dream that was her waking day,

Wherein she journeyed, borne along the ground

Without her own volition in some way,

Or fleeing, motionless, with feet fast bound,

Or running silent through a silent house

Sharply remembered from an earlier dream,

Upstairs, down other stairs, fearful to rouse,

Regarding him, the wide and empty scream

Of a strange sleeper on a malignant bed,

And all the time not certain if it were

Herself so doing or some one like to her,

From this wan dream that was her daily bread,

Sometimes, at night, incredulous, she would wake—

A child, blowing bubbles that the chairs and carpet

    did not break!

XIV

She had a horror he would die at night.

And sometimes when the light began to fade

She could not keep from noticing how white

The birches looked—and then she would be afraid,

Even with a lamp, to go about the house

And lock the windows; and as night wore on

Toward morning, if a dog howled, or a mouse

Squeaked in the floor, long after it was gone

Her flesh would sit awry on her. By day

She would forget somewhat, and it would seem

A silly thing to go with just this dream

And get a neighbor to come at night and stay.

But it would strike her sometimes, making the tea:

She had kept that kettle boiling all night long, for company.

XV

There was upon the sill a pencil mark,

Vital with shadow when the sun stood still

At noon, but now, because the day was dark,

It was a pencil mark upon the sill.

And the mute clock, maintaining ever the same

Dead moment, blank and vacant of itself,

Was a pink shepherdess, a picture frame,

A shell marked Souvenir, there on the shelf.

Whence it occurred to her that he might be,

The mainspring being broken in his mind,

A clock himself, if one were so inclined,

That stood at twenty minutes after three—

The reason being for this, it might be said,

That things in death were neither clocks nor people,
    but only dead.

XVI

The doctor asked her what she wanted done

With him, that could not lie there many days.

And she was shocked to see how life goes on

Even after death, in irritating ways;

And mused how if he had not died at all

'Twould have been easier—then there need not be

The stiff disorder of a funeral

Everywhere, and the hideous industry,

And crowds of people calling her by name

And questioning her, she'd never seen before,

But only watching by his bed once more

And sitting silent if a knocking came . . .

She said at length, feeling the doctor's eyes,

"I don't know what you do exactly when a person

    dies."

XVII

Gazing upon him now, severe and dead,
It seemed a curious thing that she had lain
Beside him many a night in that cold bed,
And that had been which would not be again.
From his desirous body the great heat
Was gone at last, it seemed, and the taut nerves
Loosened forever. Formally the sheet
Set forth for her today those heavy curves
And lengths familiar as the bedroom door.
She was as one who enters, sly, and proud,
To where her husband speaks before a crowd,
And sees a man she never saw before—
The man who eats his victuals at her side,
Small, and absurd, and hers: for once, not hers,
     unclassified.

Finis

Life, were thy pains as are the pains of hell,
So hardly to be borne, yet to be borne,
And all thy boughs more grim with wasp and thorn
Than armoured bough stood ever; too chill to spell
With the warm tongue, and sharp with broken shell
Thy ways, whereby in wincing haste forlorn
The desperate foot must travel, blind and torn,
Yet must I cry: So be it; it is well.
So fair to me thy vineyards, nor less fair
Than the sweet heaven my fathers hoped to gain;
So bright this earthly blossom spiked with care,
This harvest hung behind the boughs of pain,
Needs must I gather, guessing by the stain
I bleed, but know not wherefore, know not where.

Υ

Grow not too high, grow not too far from home,
Green tree, whose roots are in the granite's face!
Taller than silver spire or golden dome
A tree may grow above its earthy place,
And taller than a cloud, but not so tall
The root may not be mother to the stem,
Lifting rich plenty, though the rivers fall,
To the cold sunny leaves to nourish them.
Have done with blossoms for a time, be bare;
Split rock; plunge downward; take heroic soil, —
Deeper than bones, no pasture for you there;
Deeper than water, deeper than gold and oil:
Earth's fiery core alone can feed the bough
That blooms between Orion and the Plough.

Υ

Not that it matters, not that my heart's cry
Is potent to deflect our common doom,
Or bind to truce in this ambiguous room
The planets of the atom as they ply;
But only to record that you and I,
Like thieves that scratch the jewels from a tomb,
Have gathered delicate love in hardy bloom
Close under Chaos, — I rise to testify.
This is my testament: that we are taken;
Our colours are as clouds before the wind;
Yet for a moment stood the foe forsaken,
Eyeing Love's favour to our helmet pinned;
Death is our master, — but his seat is shaken;
He rides victorious, — but his ranks are thinned.

Sonnet to Gath

Country of hunchbacks!—where the strong, straight
    spine,
Jeered at by crooked children, makes his way
Through by-streets at the kindest hour of day,
Till he deplore his stature, and incline
To measure manhood with a gibbous line;
Till out of loneliness, being flawed with clay,
He stoop into his neighbour's house and say,
"Your roof is low for me—the fault is mine."
Dust in an urn long since, dispersed and dead
Is great Apollo; and the happier he;
Since who amongst you all would lift a head
At a god's radiance on the mean door-tree,
Saving to run and hide your dates and bread,
And cluck your children in about your knee?

To Inez Milholland

Read in Washington, November eighteenth, 1923, at the unveiling of a statue of three leaders in the cause of Equal Rights for Women

Upon this marble bust that is not I

Lay the round, formal wreath that is not fame;

But in the forum of my silenced cry

Root ye the living tree whose sap is flame.

I, that was proud and valiant, am no more;—

Save as a dream that wanders wide and late,

Save as a wind that rattles the stout door,

Troubling the ashes in the sheltered grate.

The stone will perish; I shall be twice dust.

Only my standard on a taken hill

Can cheat the mildew and the red-brown rust

And make immortal my adventurous will.

Even now the silk is tugging at the staff:

Take up the song; forget the epitaph.

To Jesus on His Birthday

For this your mother sweated in the cold,
For this you bled upon the bitter tree:
A yard of tinsel ribbon bought and sold;
A paper wreath; a day at home for me.
The merry bells ring out, the people kneel;
Up goes the man of God before the crowd;
With voice of honey and with eyes of steel
He drones your humble gospel to the proud.
Nobody listens. Less than the wind that blows
Are all your words to us you died to save.
O Prince of Peace! O Sharon's dewy Rose!
How mute you lie within your vaulted grave.
The stone the angel rolled away with tears
Is back upon your mouth these thousand years.

On Hearing a Symphony of Beethoven

Sweet sounds, oh, beautiful music, do not cease!
Reject me not into the world again.
With you alone is excellence and peace,
Mankind made plausible, his purpose plain.
Enchanted in your air benign and shrewd,
With limbs a-sprawl and empty faces pale,
The spiteful and the stingy and the rude
Sleep like the scullions in the fairy-tale.
This moment is the best the world can give:
The tranquil blossom on the tortured stem.
Reject me not, sweet sounds! oh, let me live,
Till Doom espy my towers and scatter them.
A city spell-bound under the aging sun,
Music my rampart, and my only one.

Fatal Interview

I

What thing is this that, built of salt and lime
And such dry motes as in the sunbeam show,
Has power upon me that do daily climb
The dustless air?—for whom those peaks of snow
Whereup the lungs of man with borrowed breath
Go labouring to a doom I may not feel,
Are but a pearled and roseate plain beneath
My wingèd helmet and my wingèd heel.
What sweet emotions neither foe nor friend
Are these that clog my flight? what thing is this
That hastening headlong to a dusty end
Dare turn upon me these proud eyes of bliss?
Up, up, my feathers!—ere I lay you by
To journey barefoot with a mortal joy.

II

This beast that rends me in the sight of all,
This love, this longing, this oblivious thing,
That has me under as the last leaves fall,
Will glut, will sicken, will be gone by spring.
The wound will heal, the fever will abate,
The knotted hurt will slacken in the breast;
I shall forget before the flickers mate
Your look that is today my east and west.
Unscathed, however, from a claw so deep
Though I should love again I shall not go:
Along my body, waking while I sleep,
Sharp to the kiss, cold to the hand as snow,
The scar of this encounter like a sword
Will lie between me and my troubled lord.

III

No lack of counsel from the shrewd and wise
How love may be acquired and how conserved
Warrants this laying bare before your eyes
My needle to your north abruptly swerved;
If I would hold you, I must hide my fears
Lest you be wanton, lead you to believe
My compass to another quarter veers,
Little surrender, lavishly receive.
But being like my mother the brown earth
Fervent and full of gifts and free from guile,
Liefer would I you loved me for my worth,
Though you should love me but a little while,
Than for a philtre any doll can brew, —
Though thus I bound you as I long to do.

IV

Nay, learnèd doctor, these fine leeches fresh
From the pond's edge my cause cannot remove:
Alas, the sick disorder in my flesh
Is deeper than your skill, is very love.
And you, good friar, far liefer would I think
Upon my dear, and dream him in your place,
Than heed your *ben'cites* and heavenward sink
With empty heart and noddle full of grace.
Breathes but one mortal on the teeming globe
Could minister to my soul's or body's needs—
Physician minus physic, minus robe;
Confessor minus Latin, minus beads.
Yet should you bid me name him, I am dumb;
For though you summon him, he would not come.

V

Of all that ever in extreme disease
"Sweet Love, sweet cruel Love, have pity!" cried,
Count me the humblest, hold me least of these
That wear the red heart crumpled in the side,
In heaviest durance, dreaming or awake,
Filling the dungeon with their piteous woe;
Not that I shriek not till the dungeon shake,
"Oh, God! Oh, let me out! Oh, let me go!"
But that my chains throughout their iron length
Make such a golden clank upon my ear,
But that I would not, boasted I the strength,
Up with a terrible arm and out of here
Where thrusts my morsel daily through the bars
This tall, oblivious gaoler eyed with stars.

VI

Since I cannot persuade you from this mood
Of pale preoccupation with the dead,
Not for my comfort nor for your own good
Shift your concern to living bones instead;
Since that which Helen did and ended Troy
Is more than I can do though I be warm,
Have up your buried girls, egregious boy,
And stand with them against the unburied storm.
When you lie wasted and your blood runs thin,
And what's to do must with dispatch be done,
Call Cressid, call Elaine, call Isolt in!—
More bland the ichor of a ghost should run
Along your dubious veins than the rude sea
Of passion pounding all day long in me.

VII

Night is my sister, and how deep in love,

How drowned in love and weedily washed ashore,

There to be fretted by the drag and shove

At the tide's edge, I lie—these things and more:

Whose arm alone between me and the sand,

Whose voice alone, whose pitiful breath brought near,

Could thaw these nostrils and unlock this hand,

She could advise you, should you care to hear.

Small chance, however, in a storm so black,

A man will leave his friendly fire and snug

For a drowned woman's sake, and bring her back

To drip and scatter shells upon the rug.

No one but Night, with tears on her dark face,

Watches beside me in this windy place.

VIII

Yet in an hour to come, disdainful dust,
You shall be bowed and brought to bed with me.
While the blood roars, or when the blood is rust
About a broken engine, this shall be.
If not today, then later; if not here
On the green grass, with sighing and delight,
Then under it, all in good time, my dear,
We shall be laid together in the night.
And ruder and more violent, be assured,
Than the desirous body's heat and sweat
That shameful kiss by more than night obscured
Wherewith at length the scornfullest mouth is met.
Life has no friend; her converts late or soon
Slide back to feed the dragon with the moon.

IX

When you are dead, and your disturbing eyes
No more as now their stormy lashes lift
To lance me through—as in the morning skies
One moment, plainly visible in a rift
Of cloud, two splendid planets may appear
And purely blaze, and are at once withdrawn,
What time the watcher in desire and fear
Leans from his chilly window in the dawn—
Shall I be free, shall I be once again
As others are, and count your loss no care?
Oh, never more, till my dissolving brain
Be powerless to evoke you out of air,
Remembered morning stars, more fiercely bright
Than all the Alphas of the actual night!

X

Strange thing that I, by nature nothing prone
To fret the summer blossom on its stem,
Who know the hidden nest, but leave alone
The magic eggs, the bird that cuddles them,
Should have no peace till your bewildered heart
Hung fluttering at the window of my breast,
Till I had ravished to my bitter smart
Your kiss from the stern moment, could not rest.
"Swift wing, sweet blossom, live again in air!
Depart, poor flower; poor feathers you are free!"
Thus do I cry, being teased by shame and care
That beauty should be brought to terms by me;
Yet shamed the more that in my heart I know,
Cry as I may, I could not let you go.

XI

Not in a silver casket cool with pearls
Or rich with red corundum or with blue,
Locked, and the key withheld, as other girls
Have given their loves, I give my love to you;
Not in a lovers'-knot, not in a ring
Worked in such fashion, and the legend plain—
Semper fidelis, where a secret spring
Kennels a drop of mischief for the brain:
Love in the open hand, no thing but that,
Ungemmed, unhidden, wishing not to hurt,
As one should bring you cowslips in a hat
Swung from the hand, or apples in her skirt,
I bring you, calling out as children do:
"Look what I have!—And these are all for you."

Olympian gods, mark now my bedside lamp
Blown out; and be advised too late that he
Whom you call sire is stolen into the camp
Of warring Earth, and lies abed with me.
Call out your golden hordes, the harm is done:
Enraptured in his great embrace I lie;
Shake heaven with spears, but I shall bear a son
Branded with godhead, heel and brow and thigh.
Whom think not to bedazzle or confound
With meteoric splendours or display
Of blackened moons or suns or the big sound
Of sudden thunder on a silent day;
Pain and compassion shall he know, being mine,—
Confusion never, that is half divine.

XIII

I said, seeing how the winter gale increased,

Even as waxed within us and grew strong

The ancient tempest of desire, "At least,

It is the season when the nights are long.

Well flown, well shattered from the summer hedge

The early sparrow and the opening flowers!—

Late climbs the sun above the southerly edge

These days, and sweet to love those added hours."

Alas, already does the dark recede,

And visible are the trees against the snow.

Oh, monstrous parting, oh, perfidious deed,

How shall I leave your side, how shall I go? . . .

Unnatural night, the shortest of the year,

Farewell! 'Tis dawn. The longest day is here.

XIV

Since of no creature living the last breath
Is twice required, or twice the ultimate pain,
Seeing how to quit your arms is very death,
'Tis likely that I shall not die again;
And likely 'tis that Time whose gross decree
Sends now the dawn to clamour at our door,
Thus having done his evil worst to me,
Will thrust me by, will harry me no more.
When you are corn and roses and at rest
I shall endure, a dense and sanguine ghost,
To haunt the scene where I was happiest,
To bend above the thing I loved the most;
And rise, and wring my hands, and steal away
As I do now, before the advancing day.

XV

My worship from this hour the Sparrow-Drawn
Alone will cherish, and her arrowy child,
Whose groves alone in the inquiring dawn
Rise tranquil, and their altars undefiled.
Seaward and shoreward smokes a plundered land
To guard whose portals was my dear employ;
Razed are its temples now; inviolate stand
Only the slopes of Venus and her boy.
How have I stripped me of immortal aid
Save theirs alone, — who could endure to see
Forsworn Aeneas with conspiring blade
Sever the ship from shore (alas for me)
And make no sign; who saw, and did not speak,
The brooch of Troilus pinned upon the Greek.

XVI

I dreamed I moved among the Elysian fields,
In converse with sweet women long since dead;
And out of blossoms which that meadow yields
I wove a garland for your living head.
Danae, that was the vessel for a day
Of golden Jove, I saw, and at her side,
Whom Jove the Bull desired and bore away,
Europa stood, and the Swan's featherless bride.
All these were mortal women, yet all these
Above the ground had had a god for guest;
Freely I walked beside them and at ease,
Addressing them, by them again addressed,
And marvelled nothing, for remembering you,
Wherefore I was among them well I knew.

XVII

Sweet love, sweet thorn, when lightly to my heart
I took your thrust, whereby I since am slain,
And lie disheveled in the grass apart,
A sodden thing bedrenched by tears and rain,
While rainy evening drips to misty night,
And misty night to cloudy morning clears,
And clouds disperse across the gathering light,
And birds grow noisy, and the sun appears—
Had I bethought me then, sweet love, sweet thorn,
How sharp an anguish even at the best,
When all's requited and the future sworn,
The happy hour can leave within the breast,
I had not so come running at the call
Of one who loves me little, if at all.

XVIII

Shall I be prisoner till my pulses stop

To hateful Love and drag his noisy chain,

And bait my need with sugared crusts that drop

From jeweled fingers neither kind nor clean?—

Mewed in an airless cavern where a toad

Would grieve to snap his gnat and lay him down,

While in the light along the rattling road

Men shout and chaff and drive their wares to town? . . .

Perfidious Prince, that keep me here confined,

Doubt not I know the letters of my doom:

How many a man has left his blood behind

To buy his exit from this mournful room

These evil stains record, these walls that rise

Carved with his torment, steamy with his sighs.

XIX

My most distinguished guest and learnèd friend,

The pallid hare that runs before the day

Having brought your earnest counsels to an end

Now have I somewhat of my own to say:

That it is folly to be sunk in love,

And madness plain to make the matter known,

These are no mysteries you are verger of;

Everyman's wisdoms these are, and my own.

If I have flung my heart unto a hound

I have done ill, it is a certain thing;

Yet breathe I freer, walk I the more sound

On my sick bones for this brave reasoning?

Soon must I say, "'Tis prowling Death I hear!"

Yet come no better off, for my quick ear.

XX

Think not, nor for a moment let your mind,
Wearied with thinking, doze upon the thought
That the work's done and the long day behind,
And beauty, since 'tis paid for, can be bought.
If in the moonlight from the silent bough
Suddenly with precision speak your name
The nightingale, be not assured that now
His wing is limed and his wild virtue tame.
Beauty beyond all feathers that have flown
Is free; you shall not hood her to your wrist,
Nor sting her eyes, nor have her for your own
In any fashion; beauty billed and kissed
Is not your turtle; tread her like a dove —
She loves you not; she never heard of love.

XXI

Gone in good sooth you are: not even in dream
You come. As if the strictures of the light,
Laid on our glances to their disesteem,
Extended even to shadows and the night;

Extended even beyond that drowsy sill
Along whose galleries open to the skies
All maskers move unchallenged and at will,
Visor in hand or hooded to the eyes.

To that pavilion the green sea in flood
Curves in, and the slow dancers dance in foam;
I find again the pink camellia-bud
On the wide step, beside a silver comb. . . .

But it is scentless; up the marble stair
I mount with pain, knowing you are not there.

XXII

Now by this moon, before this moon shall wane
I shall be dead or I shall be with you!
No moral concept can outweigh the pain
Past rack and wheel this absence puts me through;
Faith, honour, pride, endurance, what the tongues
Of tedious men will say, or what the law—
For which of these do I fill up my lungs
With brine and fire at every breath I draw?
Time, and to spare, for patience by and by,
Time to be cold and time to sleep alone;
Let me no more until the hour I die
Defraud my innocent senses of their own.
Before this moon shall darken, say of me:
She's in her grave, or where she wants to be.

XXIII

I know the face of Falsehood and her tongue
Honeyed with unction, plausible with guile,
Are dear to men, whom count me not among,
That owe their daily credit to her smile;
Such have been succoured out of great distress
By her contriving, if accounts be true:
Their deference now above the board, I guess,
Discharges what beneath the board is due.
As for myself, I'd liefer lack her aid
Than eat her presence; let this building fall:
But let me never lift my latch, afraid
To hear her simpering accents in the hall,
Nor force an entrance past mephitic airs
Of stale patchouli hanging on my stairs.

XXIV

Whereas at morning in a jeweled crown

I bit my fingers and was hard to please,

Having shook disaster till the fruit fell down

I feel tonight more happy and at ease:

Feet running in the corridors, men quick-

Buckling their sword-belts bumping down the stair,

Challenge, and rattling bridge-chain, and the click

Of hooves on pavement—this will clear the air.

Private this chamber as it has not been

In many a month of muffled hours; almost,

Lulled by the uproar, I could lie serene

And sleep, until all's won, until all's lost,

And the door's opened and the issue shown,

And I walk forth Hell's mistress . . . or my own.

XXV

Peril upon the paths of this desire

Lies like the natural darkness of the night,

For me unpeopled; let him hence retire

Whom as a child a shadow could affright;

And fortune speed him from this dubious place

Where roses blenched or blackened of their hue,

Pallid and stemless float on undulant space,

Or clustered hidden shock the hand with dew.

Whom as a child the night's obscurity

Did not alarm, let him alone remain,

Lanterned but by the longing in the eye,

And warmed but by the fever in the vein,

To lie with me, sentried from wrath and scorn

By sleepless Beauty and her polished thorn.

XXVI

Women have loved before as I love now;
At least, in lively chronicles of the past—
Of Irish waters by a Cornish prow
Or Trojan waters by a Spartan mast
Much to their cost invaded—here and there,
Hunting the amorous line, skimming the rest,
I find some woman bearing as I bear
Love like a burning city in the breast.
I think however that of all alive
I only in such utter, ancient way
Do suffer love; in me alone survive
The unregenerate passions of a day
When treacherous queens, with death upon the tread,
Heedless and wilful, took their knights to bed.

XXVII

Moon, that against the lintel of the west
Your forehead lean until the gate be swung,
Longing to leave the world and be at rest,
Being worn with faring and no longer young,
Do you recall at all the Carian hill
Where worn with loving, loving late you lay,
Halting the sun because you lingered still,
While wondering candles lit the Carian day?
Ah, if indeed this memory to your mind
Recall some sweet employment, pity me,
That with the dawn must leave my love behind,
That even now the dawn's dim herald see!
I charge you, goddess, in the name of one
You loved as well: endure, hold off the sun.

XXVIII

When we are old and these rejoicing veins
Are frosty channels to a muted stream,
And out of all our burning there remains
No feeblest spark to fire us, even in dream,
This be our solace: that it was not said
When we were young and warm and in our prime,
Upon our couch we lay as lie the dead,
Sleeping away the unreturning time.
O sweet, O heavy-lidded, O my love,
When morning strikes her spear upon the land,
And we must rise and arm us and reprove
The insolent daylight with a steady hand,
Be not discountenanced if the knowing know
We rose from rapture but an hour ago.

XXIX

Heart, have no pity on this house of bone:

Shake it with dancing, break it down with joy.

No man holds mortgage on it; it is your own;

To give, to sell at auction, to destroy.

When you are blind to moonlight on the bed,

When you are deaf to gravel on the pane,

Shall quavering caution from this house instead

Cluck forth at summer mischief in the lane?

All that delightful youth forbears to spend

Molestful age inherits, and the ground

Will have us; therefore, while we're young, my friend—

The Latin's vulgar, but the advice is sound.

Youth, have no pity; leave no farthing here

For age to invest in compromise and fear.

XXX

Love is not all: it is not meat nor drink
Nor slumber nor a roof against the rain;
Nor yet a floating spar to men that sink
And rise and sink and rise and sink again;
Love can not fill the thickened lung with breath,
Nor clean the blood, nor set the fractured bone;
Yet many a man is making friends with death
Even as I speak, for lack of love alone.
It well may be that in a difficult hour,
Pinned down by pain and moaning for release,
Or nagged by want past resolution's power,
I might be driven to sell your love for peace,
Or trade the memory of this night for food.
It well may be. I do not think I would.

XXXI

When we that wore the myrtle wear the dust,
And years of darkness cover up our eyes,
And all our arrogant laughter and sweet lust
Keep counsel with the scruples of the wise;
When boys and girls that now are in the loins
Of croaking lads, dip oar into the sea, —
And who are these that dive for copper coins?
No longer we, my love, no longer we—
Then let the fortunate breathers of the air,
When we lie speechless in the muffling mould,
Tease not our ghosts with slander, pause not there
To say that love is false and soon grows cold,
But pass in silence the mute grave of two
Who lived and died believing love was true.

XXXII

Time, that is pleased to lengthen out the day

For grieving lovers parted or denied,

And pleased to hurry the sweet hours away

From such as lie enchanted side by side,

Is not my kinsman; nay, my feudal foe

Is he that in my childhood was the thief

Of all my mother's beauty, and in woe

My father bowed, and brought our house to grief.

Thus, though he think to touch with hateful frost

Your treasured curls, and your clear forehead line,

And so persuade me from you, he has lost;

Never shall he inherit what was mine.

When Time and all his tricks have done their worst,

Still will I hold you dear, and him accurst.

XXXIII

Sorrowful dreams remembered after waking
Shadow with dolour all the candid day;
Even as I read, the silly tears out-breaking
Splash on my hands and shut the page away. . . .
Grief at the root, a dark and secret dolour,
Harder to bear than wind-and-weather grief,
Clutching the rose, draining its cheek of colour,
Drying the bud, curling the opened leaf.
Deep is the pond—although the edge be shallow,
Frank in the sun, revealing fish and stone,
Climbing ashore to turtle-head and mallow—
Black at the centre beats a heart unknown.
Desolate dreams pursue me out of sleep;
Weeping I wake; waking, I weep, I weep.

XXXIV

Most wicked words! forbear to speak them out.

Utter them not again; blaspheme no more

Against our love with maxims learned from Doubt:

Lest Death should get his foot inside the door.

We are surrounded by a hundred foes;

And he that at your bidding joins our feast,

I stake my heart upon it, is one of those,

Nor in their councils does he sit the least.

Hark not his whisper: he is Time's ally,

Kinsman to Death, and leman of Despair:

Believe that I shall love you till I die;

Believe; and thrust him forth; and arm the stair;

And top the walls with spikes and splintered glass

That he pass gutted should again he pass.

XXXV

Clearly my ruined garden as it stood

Before the frost came on it I recall—

Stiff marigolds, and what a trunk of wood

The zinnia had, that was the first to fall;

These pale and oozy stalks, these hanging leaves

Nerveless and darkened, dripping in the sun,

Cannot gainsay me, though the spirit grieves

And wrings its hands at what the frost has done.

If in a widening silence you should guess

I read the moment with recording eyes,

Taking your love and all your loveliness

Into a listening body hushed of sighs . . .

Though summer's rife and the warm rose in season,

Rebuke me not: I have a winter reason.

XXXVI

Hearing your words, and not a word among them
Tuned to my liking, on a salty day
When inland woods were pushed by winds that flung
    them
Hissing to leeward like a ton of spray,
I thought how off Matinicus the tide
Came pounding in, came running through the Gut,
While from the Rock the warning whistle cried,
And children whimpered, and the doors blew shut;
There in the autumn when the men go forth,
With slapping skirts the island women stand
In gardens stripped and scattered, peering north,
With dahlia tubers dripping from the hand:
The wind of their endurance, driving south,
Flattened your words against your speaking mouth.

XXXVII

Believe, if ever the bridges of this town,

Whose towers were builded without fault or stain,

Be taken, and its battlements go down,

No mortal roof shall shelter me again;

I shall not prop a branch against a bough

To hide me from the whipping east or north,

Nor tease to flame a heap of sticks, who now

Am warmed by all the wonders of the earth.

Do you take ship unto some happier shore

In such event, and have no thought for me,

I shall remain;—to share the ruinous floor

With roofs that once were seen far out at sea;

To cheer a mouldering army on the march . . .

And beg from spectres by a broken arch.

XXXVIII

You say: "Since life is cruel enough at best;"

You say: "Considering how our love is cursed,

And housed so bleakly that the sea-gull's nest

Were better shelter, even as better nursed

Between the breaker and the stingy reeds

Ragged and coarse that hiss against the sand

The gull's brown chick, and hushed in all his needs,

Than our poor love so harried through the land—

You being too tender, even with all your scorn,

To line his cradle with the world's reproof,

And I too devious, too surrendered, born

Too far from home to hunt him even a roof

Out of the rain—" Oh, tortured voice, be still!

Spare me your premise: leave me when you will.

XXXIX

Love me no more, now let the god depart,
If love be grown so bitter to your tongue!
Here is my hand; I bid you from my heart
Fare well, fare very well, be always young.
As for myself, mine was a deeper drouth:
I drank and thirsted still; but I surmise
My kisses now are sand against your mouth,
Teeth in your palm and pennies on your eyes.
Speak but one cruel word, to shame my tears;
Go, but in going, stiffen up my back
To meet the yelping of the mustering years—
Dim, trotting shapes that seldom will attack
Two with a light who match their steps and sing:
To one alone and lost, another thing.

XL

You loved me not at all, but let it go;

I loved you more than life, but let it be.

As the more injured party, this being so,

The hour's amenities are all to me—

The choice of weapons; and I gravely choose

To let the weapons tarnish where they lie;

And spend the night in eloquent abuse

Of senators and popes and such small fry

And meet the morning standing, and at odds

With heaven and earth and hell and any fool

Who calls his soul his own, and all the gods,

And all the children getting dressed for school . . .

And you will leave me, and I shall entomb

What's cold by then in an adjoining room.

XLI

I said in the beginning, did I not?—
Prophetic of the end, though unaware
How light you took me, ignorant that you thought
I spoke to see my breath upon the air:
If you walk east at daybreak from the town
To the cliff's foot, by climbing steadily
You cling at noon whence there is no way down
But to go toppling backward to the sea.
And not for birds nor birds'-eggs, so they say,
But for a flower that in these fissures grows,
Forms have been seen to move throughout the day
Skyward; but what its name is no one knows.
'Tis said you find beside them on the sand
This flower, relinquished by the broken hand.

XLII

O ailing Love, compose your struggling wing!

Confess you mortal; be content to die.

How better dead, than be this awkward thing

Dragging in dust its feathers of the sky;

Hitching and rearing, plunging beak to loam,

Upturned, disheveled, uttering a weak sound

Less proud than of the gull that rakes the foam,

Less kind than of the hawk that scours the ground.

While yet your awful beauty, even at bay,

Beats off the impious eye, the outstretched hand,

And what your hue or fashion none can say,

Vanish, be fled, leave me a wingless land . . .

Save where one moment down the quiet tide

Fades a white swan, with a black swan beside.

XLIII

Summer, be seen no more within this wood;

Nor you, red Autumn, down its paths appear;

Let no more the false mitrewort intrude

Nor the dwarf cornel nor the gentian here;

You too be absent, unavailing Spring,

Nor let those thrushes that with pain conspire

From out this wood their wild arpeggios fling,

Shaking the nerves with memory and desire.

Only that season which is no man's friend,

You, surly Winter, in this wood be found;

Freeze up the year; with sleet these branches bend

Though rasps the locust in the fields around.

Now darken, sky! Now shrieking blizzard, blow!—

Farewell, sweet bank; be blotted out with snow.

If to be left were to be left alone,

And lock the door and find one's self again—

Drag forth and dust Penates of one's own

That in a corner all too long have lain;

Read Brahms, read Chaucer, set the chessmen out

In classic problem, stretch the shrunken mind

Back to its stature on the rack of thought—

Loss might be said to leave its boon behind.

But fruitless conference and the interchange

With callow wits of bearded *cons* and *pros*

Enlist the neutral daylight, and derange

A will too sick to battle for repose.

Neither with you nor with myself, I spend

Loud days that have no meaning and no end.

XLV

I know my mind and I have made my choice;
Not from your temper does my doom depend;
Love me or love me not, you have no voice
In this, which is my portion to the end.
Your presence and your favours, the full part
That you could give, you now can take away:
What lies between your beauty and my heart
Not even you can trouble or betray.
Mistake me not—unto my inmost core
I do desire your kiss upon my mouth;
They have not craved a cup of water more
That bleach upon the deserts of the south;
Here might you bless me; what you cannot do
Is bow me down, who have been loved by you.

Even in the moment of our earliest kiss,

When sighed the straitened bud into the flower,

Sat the dry seed of most unwelcome this;

And that I knew, though not the day and hour.

Too season-wise am I, being country-bred,

To tilt at autumn or defy the frost:

Snuffing the chill even as my fathers did,

I say with them, "What's out tonight is lost."

I only hoped, with the mild hope of all

Who watch the leaf take shape upon the tree,

A fairer summer and a later fall

Than in these parts a man is apt to see,

And sunny clusters ripened for the wine:

I tell you this across the blackened vine.

XLVII

Well, I have lost you; and I lost you fairly;

In my own way, and with my full consent.

Say what you will, kings in a tumbrel rarely

Went to their deaths more proud than this one went.

Some nights of apprehension and hot weeping

I will confess; but that's permitted me;

Day dried my eyes; I was not one for keeping

Rubbed in a cage a wing that would be free.

If I had loved you less or played you slyly

I might have held you for a summer more,

But at the cost of words I value highly,

And no such summer as the one before.

Should I outlive this anguish—and men do—

I shall have only good to say of you.

XLVIII

Now by the path I climbed, I journey back.

The oaks have grown; I have been long away.

Taking with me your memory and your lack

I now descend into a milder day;

Stripped of your love, unburdened of my hope,

Descend the path I mounted from the plain;

Yet steeper than I fancied seems the slope

And stonier, now that I go down again.

Warm falls the dusk; the clanking of a bell

Faintly ascends upon this heavier air;

I do recall those grassy pastures well:

In early spring they drove the cattle there.

And close at hand should be a shelter, too,

From which the mountain peaks are not in view.

XLIX

There is a well into whose bottomless eye,
Though I were flayed, I dare not lean and look,
Sweet once with mountain water, now gone dry,
Miraculously abandoned by the brook
Wherewith for years miraculously fed
It kept a constant level cold and bright,
Though summer parched the rivers in their bed;
Withdrawn these waters, vanished overnight.
There is a word I dare not speak again,
A face I never again must call to mind;
I was not craven ever nor blenched at pain,
But pain to such degree and of such kind
As I must suffer if I think of you,
Not in my senses will I undergo.

L

The heart once broken is a heart no more,
And is absolved from all a heart must be;
All that it signed or chartered heretofore
Is cancelled now, the bankrupt heart is free;
So much of duty as you may require
Of shards and dust, this and no more of pain,
This and no more of hope, remorse, desire,
The heart once broken need support again.
How simple 'tis, and what a little sound
It makes in breaking, let the world attest:
It struggles, and it fails; the world goes round,
And the moon follows it. Heart in my breast,
'Tis half a year now since you broke in two;
The world's forgotten well, if the world knew.

LI

If in the years to come you should recall,

When faint at heart or fallen on hungry days,

Or full of griefs and little if at all

From them distracted by delights or praise;

When failing powers or good opinion lost

Have bowed your neck, should you recall to mind

How of all men I honoured you the most,

Holding you noblest among mortal-kind:

Might not my love—although the curving blade

From whose wide mowing none may hope to hide,

Me long ago below the frosts had laid—

Restore you somewhat to your former pride?

Indeed I think this memory, even then,

Must raise you high among the run of men.

LII

Oh, sleep forever in the Latmian cave,
Mortal Endymion, darling of the Moon!
Her silver garments by the senseless wave
Shouldered and dropped and on the shingle strewn,
Her fluttering hand against her forehead pressed,
Her scattered looks that trouble all the sky,
Her rapid footsteps running down the west—
Of all her altered state, oblivious lie!
Whom earthen you, by deathless lips adored,
Wild-eyed and stammering to the grasses thrust,
And deep into her crystal body poured
The hot and sorrowful sweetness of the dust:
Whereof she wanders mad, being all unfit
For mortal love, that might not die of it.

Finis

Two Sonnets in Memory

(NICOLA SACCO—BARTOLOMEO VANZETTI)
Executed August 23, 1927

I

As men have loved their lovers in times past

And sung their wit, their virtue and their grace,

So have we loved sweet Justice to the last,

Who now lies here in an unseemly place.

The child will quit the cradle and grow wise

And stare on beauty till his senses drown;

Yet shall be seen no more by mortal eyes

Such beauty as here walked and here went down.

Like birds that hear the winter crying plain

Her courtiers leave to seek the clement south;

Many have praised her, we alone remain

To break a fist against the lying mouth

Of any man who says this was not so:

Though she be dead now, as indeed we know.

II

Where can the heart be hidden in the ground
And be at peace, and be at peace forever,
Under the world, untroubled by the sound
Of mortal tears, that cease from pouring never?
Well for the heart, by stern compassion harried,
If death be deeper than the churchmen say, —
Gone from this world indeed what's graveward carried,
And laid to rest indeed what's laid away.
Anguish enough while yet the indignant breather
Have blood to spurt upon the oppressor's hand;
Who would eternal be, and hang in ether
A stuffless ghost above his struggling land,
Retching in vain to render up the groan
That is not there, being aching dust's alone?

Υ

Time, that renews the tissues of this frame,

That built the child and hardened the soft bone,

Taught him to wail, to blink, to walk alone,

Stare, question, wonder, give the world a name,

Forget the watery darkness whence he came,

Attends no less the boy to manhood grown,

Brings him new raiment, strips him of his own;

All skins are shed at length, remorse, even shame.

Such hope is mine, if this indeed be true,

I dread no more the first white in my hair,

Or even age itself, the easy shoe,

The cane, the wrinkled hands, the special chair:

Time, doing this to me, may alter too

My sorrow, into something I can bear.

Υ

I too beneath your moon, almighty Sex,

Go forth at nightfall crying like a cat,

Leaving the lofty tower I laboured at

For birds to foul and boys and girls to vex

With tittering chalk; and you, and the long necks

Of neighbours sitting where their mothers sat

Are well aware of shadowy this and that

In me, that's neither noble nor complex.

Such as I am, however, I have brought

To what it is, this tower; it is my own;

Though it was reared To Beauty, it was wrought

From what I had to build with: honest bone

Is there, and anguish; pride; and burning thought;

And lust is there, and nights not spent alone.

Y

Now from a stout and more imperious day
Let dead impatience arm me for the act.
We bear too much. Let the proud past gainsay
This tolerance. Now, upon the sleepy pact
That bound us two as lovers, now in the night
And ebb of love, let me with stealth proceed,
Catch the vow nodding, harden, feel no fright,
Bring forth the weapon sleekly, do the deed.
I know—and having seen, shall not deny—
This flag inverted keeps its colour still;
This moon in wane and scooped against the sky
Blazes in stern reproach. Stare back, my Will—
We can out-gaze it; we can do better yet:
We can expunge it. I will not watch it set.

Υ

When did I ever deny, though this was fleeting,
That this was love? When did I ever, I say,
With iron thumb put out the eyes of day
In this cold world where charity lies bleating
Under a thorn, and none to give him greeting,
And all that lights endeavour on its way
Is the teased lamp of loving, the torn ray
Of the least kind, the most clandestine meeting?
As God's my judge, I do cry holy, holy,
Upon the name of love however brief,
For want of whose ill-trimmed, aspiring wick
More days than one I have gone forward slowly
In utter dark, scuffling the drifted leaf,
Tapping the road before me with a stick.

Υ

Thou famished grave, I will not fill thee yet,
Roar though thou dost, I am too happy here;
Gnaw thine own sides, fast on; I have no fear
Of thy dark project, but my heart is set
On living—I have heroes to beget
Before I die; I will not come anear
Thy dismal jaws for many a splendid year;
Till I be old, I aim not to be eat.
I cannot starve thee out: I am thy prey
And thou shalt have me; but I dare defend
That I can stave thee off; and I dare say,
What with the life I lead, the force I spend,
I'll be but bones and jewels on that day,
And leave thee hungry even in the end.

Υ

Now that the west is washed of clouds and clear,
The sun gone under and his beams laid by,
You, that require a quarter of the sky
To shine alone in: prick the dust, appear,
Beautiful Venus! The dense atmosphere
Cannot diffuse your rays, you blaze so high,
Lighting with loveliness a crisp and dry
Cold evening in the autumn of the year.
The pilot standing by his broken plane
In the unheard-of mountains, looks on you,
And warms his heart a moment at your light . . .
Benignant planet, sweet, familiar sight . . .
Thinking he may be found, he may again
See home, breaks the stale buttered crust in two.

To Elinor Wylie

Oh, she was beautiful in every part! —

The auburn hair that bound the subtle brain;

The lovely mouth cut clear by wit and pain,

Uttering oaths and nonsense, uttering art

In casual speech and curving at the smart

On startled ears of excellence too plain

For early morning! — *Obit.* Death from strain;

The soaring mind outstripped the tethered heart.

Yet here was one who had no need to die

To be remembered. Every word she said,

The lively malice of the hazel eye

Scanning the thumb-nail close — oh, dazzling dead,

How like a comet through the darkening sky

You raced! . . . would your return were heralded.

Υ

Enormous moon, that rise behind these hills
Heavy and yellow in a sky unstarred
And pale, your girth by purple fillets barred
Of drifting cloud, that as the cool sky fills
With planets and the brighter stars, distills
To thinnest vapour and floats valley-ward,
You flood with radiance all this cluttered yard,
The sagging fence, the chipping window sills.
Grateful at heart as if for my delight
You rose, I watch you through a mist of tears,
Thinking how man, who gags upon despair,
Salting his hunger with the sweat of fright
Has fed on cold indifference all these years,
Calling it kindness, calling it God's care.

Υ

Be sure my coming was a sharp offense

And trouble to my mother in her bed;

And harsh to me must be my going hence,

Though I were old and spent and better dead;

Between the awful spears of birth and death

I run a grassy gauntlet in the sun;

And curdled in me is my central pith,

Remembering there is dying to be done.

O Life, my little day, at what a cost

Have you been purchased! What a bargain's here!

(And yet, thou canny Lender, thou hast lost:

Thumb thy fat book until my debt appear:

So . . . art thou stuck? . . . thou canst not strike that
    through

For the small dying that a man can do!)

Υ

Now let the mouth of wailing for a time
Be shut, ye happy mourners; and return
To the marked door, the ribbon and the fern,
Without a tear. The good man in his prime,
The pretty child, the Gone—from a fair clime
Above the ashes of the solemn urn
Behold you; wherefore, then, these hearts that burn
With hot remorse, these cheeks the tears begrime?
Grief that is grief and worthy of that word
Is ours alone for whom no hope can be
That the loved eyes look down and understand.
Ye true believers, trusters in the Lord,
Today bereft, tomorrow hand in hand,
Think ye not shame to show your tears to me?

Y

Not only love plus awful grief,
The ardent and consuming pain
Of all who loved and who remain
To tend alone the buried brief
Eternal, propping laurel-leaf
And frozen rose above the slain, —
But pity lest they die again
Makes of the mind an iron sheaf
Of bundled memories. Ah, bright ghost,
Who shadow all I have and do,
Be gracious in your turn, be gone!
Suffice it that I loved you most.
I would be rid of even you,
And see the world I look upon.

Czecho-Slovakia

If there were balm in Gilead, I would go
To Gilead for your wounds, unhappy land,
Gather you balsam there, and with this hand,
Made deft by pity, cleanse and bind and sew
And drench with healing, that your strength might
    grow,
(Though love be outlawed, kindness contraband)
And you, O proud and felled, again might stand;
But where to look for balm, I do not know.
The oils and herbs of mercy are so few;
Honour's for sale; allegiance has its price;
The barking of a fox has bought us all;
We save our skins a craven hour or two. —
While Peter warms him in the servants' hall
The thorns are platted and the cock crows twice.

Υ

Count them unclean, these tears that turn no mill,
This salty flux of sorrow from the heart;
Count them unclean, and grant me one day still
To weep, in an avoided room apart.
I shall come forth at length with reddened lid
Transparent, and thick mouth, and take the plough . . .
That other men may hope, as I once did;
That other men may weep, as I do now.
I am beside you, I am at your back
Firing our bridges, I am in your van;
I share your march, your hunger; all I lack
Is the sure song I cannot sing, you can.
You think we build a world; I think we leave
Only these tools, wherewith to strain and grieve.

Three Sonnets in Tetrameter

I

See how these masses mill and swarm
And troop and muster and assail:
God!—We could keep this planet warm
By friction, if the sun should fail.
Mercury, Saturn, Venus, Mars:
If no prow cuts your arid seas,
Then in your weightless air no wars
Explode with such catastrophes
As rock our planet all but loose
From its frayed mooring to the sun.
Law will not sanction such abuse
Forever; when the mischief's done,
Planets, rejoice, on which at night
Rains but the twelve-ton meteorite.

II

His stalk the dark delphinium
Unthorned into the tending hand
Releases . . . yet that hour will come . . .
And must, in such a spiny land.

The silky, powdery mignonette
Before these gathering dews are gone
May pierce me—does the rose regret
The day she did her armour on?

In that the foul supplants the fair,
The coarse defeats the twice-refined,
Is food for thought, but not despair:
All will be easier when the mind
To meet the brutal age has grown
An iron cortex of its own.

III

No further from me than my hand
Is China that I loved so well;
Love does not help to understand
The logic of the bursting shell.

Perfect in dream above me yet
Shines the white cone of Fuji-San;
I wake in fear, and weep and sweat . . .
Weep for Yoshida, for Japan.

Logic alone, all love laid by,
Must calm this crazed and plunging star:
Sorrowful news for such as I,
Who hoped—with men just as they are,
Sinful and loving—to secure
A human peace that might endure.

Υ

Upon this age, that never speaks its mind,
This furtive age, this age endowed with power
To wake the moon with footsteps, fit an oar
Into the rowlocks of the wind, and find
What swims before his prow, what swirls behind—
Upon this gifted age, in its dark hour,
Rains from the sky a meteoric shower
Of facts . . . they lie unquestioned, uncombined.
Wisdom enough to leech us of our ill
Is daily spun; but there exists no loom
To weave it into fabric; undefiled
Proceeds pure Science, and has her say; but still
Upon this world from the collective womb
Is spewed all day the red triumphant child.

Υ

My earnestness, which might at first offend,
Forgive me, for the duty it implies:
I am the convoy to the cloudy end
Of a most bright and regal enterprise;
Which under angry constellations, ill–
Mounted and under-rationed and unspurred,
Set forth to find if any country still
Might do obeisance to an honest word.
Duped and delivered up to rascals; bound
And bleeding, and his mouth stuffed; on his knees;
Robbed and imprisoned; and adjudged unsound;
I have beheld my master, if you please.
Forgive my earnestness, who at his side
Received his swift instructions, till he died.

Υ

I must not die of pity; I must live;

Grow strong, not sicken; eat, digest my food,

That it may build me, and in doing good

To blood and bone, broaden the sensitive

Fastidious pale perception: we contrive

Lean comfort for the starving, who intrude

Upon them with our pots of pity; brewed

From stronger meat must be the broth we give.

Blue, bright September day, with here and there

On the green hills a maple turning red,

And white clouds racing in the windy air! —

If I would help the weak, I must be fed

In wit and purpose, pour away despair

And rinse the cup, eat happiness like bread.

Υ

How innocent of me and my dark pain
In the clear east, unclouded save for one
Flamingo-coloured feather, combed and spun
Into fine spirals, with ephemeral stain
To dye the morning rose after the rain,
Rises the simple and majestic sun,
His azure course, well-known and often-run
With patient brightness to pursue again.
The gods are patient; they are slaves of Time
No less than we, and longer, at whose call
Must Phoebus rise and mount his dewy car,
And lift the reins and start the ancient climb;
Could we learn patience, though day-creatures all,
Our day should see us godlier than we are.

Υ

Those hours when happy hours were my estate,—
Entailed, as proper, for the next in line,
Yet mine the harvest, and the title mine—
Those acres, fertile, and the furrow straight,
From which the lark would rise—all of my late
Enchantments, still, in brilliant colours, shine,
But striped with black, the tulip, lawn and vine,
Like gardens looked at through an iron gate.
Yet not as one who never sojourned there
I view the lovely segments of a past
I lived with all my senses, well aware
That this was perfect, and it would not last:
I smell the flower, though vacuum-still the air;
I feel its texture, though the gate is fast.

Υ

Not, to me, less lavish—though my dreams have been
    splendid—
Than dreams, have been the hours of the actual day:
Never, awaking, did I awake to say:
"Nothing could be like that," when a dream was ended.
Colours, in dream; ecstasy, in dream extended
Beyond the edge of sleep—these, in their way,
Approach, come even close, yet pause, yet stay,
In the high presence of request by its answer attended.
Music, and painting, poetry, love, and grief,
Had they been more intense, I could not have borne,—
Yet, not, I think, through stout endurance lacked;
Rather, because the budding and the falling leaf
Were one, and wonderful,—not to be torn
Apart: I ask of dream: seem like the fact.

Y

Tranquility at length, when autumn comes,
Will lie upon the spirit like that haze
Touching far islands on fine autumn days
With tenderest blue, like bloom on purple plums;
Harvest will ring, but not as summer hums,
With noisy enterprise—to broaden, raise,
Proceed, proclaim, establish: autumn stays
The marching year one moment; stills the drums.

Then sits the insistent cricket in the grass;
But on the gravel crawls the chilly bee;
And all is over that could come to pass
Last year; excepting this: the mind is free
One moment, to compute, refute, amass,
Catalogue, question, contemplate, and see.

Sonnet in Dialectic

And is indeed truth beauty?—at the cost
Of all else that we cared for, can this be?—
To see the coarse triumphant, and to see
Honour and pity ridiculed, and tossed
Upon a poked-at fire; all courage lost
Save what is whelped and fattened by decree
To move among the unsuspecting free
And trap the thoughtful, with their thoughts engrossed?
Drag yet that stream for Beauty, if you will;
And find her, if you can; finding her drowned
Will not dismay your ethics,—you will still
To one and all insist she has been found . . .
And haggard men will smile your praise, until,
Some day, they stumble on her burial-mound.

Υ

To hold secure the province of Pure Art, —
What if the crude and weighty task were mine? —
For him who runs, cutting the pen less fine
Than formerly, and in the indignant heart
Dipping it straight? (to issue thence a dart,
And shine no more except as weapons shine)
The deeply-loved, the laboured, polished line
Eschew for ever? — this to be my part?
Attacked that Temple is which must not fall —
Under whose ancient shade Calliope,
Thalia, Euterpe, the nine Muses all
Went once about their happy business free:
Could I but write the Writing on the Wall! —
What matter, if one poet cease to be.

Υ

And if I die, because that part of me
Which part alone of me had chance to live,
Chose to be honour's threshing-floor, a sieve
Where right through wrong might make its way,
    and be;
If from all taint of indignation, free
Must be my art, and thereby fugitive
From all that threatens it—why—let me give
To moles my dubious immortality.
For, should I cancel by one passionate screed
All that in chaste reflection I have writ,
So that again not ever in bright need
A man shall want my verse and reach for it,
I and my verses will be dead indeed,—
That which we died to champion, hurt no whit.

Y

It is the fashion now to wave aside
As tedious, obvious, vacuous, trivial, trite,
All things which do not tickle, tease, excite
To some subversion, or in verbiage hide
Intent, or mock, or with hot sauce provide
A dish to prick the thickened appetite;
Straightforwardness is wrong, evasion right;
It is correct, *de rigueur*, to deride.
What fumy wits these modern wags expose,
For all their versatility: Voltaire,
Who wore to bed a night-cap, and would close,
In fear of drafts, all windows, could declare
In antique stuffiness, a phrase that blows
Still through men's smoky minds, and clears the air.

Alcestis to her husband, just before,
with his tearful approbation, she dies
in order that he may live.

Admetus, from my marrow's core I do

Despise you: wherefore pity not your wife,

Who, having seen expire her love for you

With heaviest grief, today gives up her life.

You could not with your mind imagine this:

One might surrender, yet continue proud.

Not having loved, you do not know: the kiss

You sadly beg, is impious, not allowed.

Of all I loved,—how many girls and men

Have loved me in return?—speak!—young or old—

Speak!—sleek or famished, can you find me then

One form would flank me, as this night grows cold?

I am at peace, Admetus—go and slake

Your grief with wine. I die for my own sake.

Y

What chores these churls do put upon the great,
What chains, what harness; the unfettered mind,
At dawn, in all directions flying blind
Yet certain, might accomplish, might create
What all men must consult or contemplate, —
Save that the spirit, earth-born and born kind,
Cannot forget small questions left behind,
Nor honest human impulse underrate:
Oh, how the speaking pen has been impeded,
To its own cost and to the cost of speech,
By specious hands that for some thinly-needed
Answer or autograph, would claw a breach
In perfect thought . . . till broken thought receded
And ebbed in foam, like ocean down a beach.

Υ

I will put Chaos into fourteen lines
And keep him there; and let him thence escape
If he be lucky; let him twist, and ape
Flood, fire, and demon—his adroit designs
Will strain to nothing in the strict confines
Of this sweet Order, where, in pious rape,
I hold his essence and amorphous shape,
Till he with Order mingles and combines.
Past are the hours, the years, of our duress,
His arrogance, our awful servitude:
I have him. He is nothing more nor less
Than something simple not yet understood;
I shall not even force him to confess;
Or answer. I will only make him good.

Υ

Come home, victorious wounded!—let the dead,
The out-of-it, the more victorious still,
Hold in the cold the hot-contested hill,
Hold by the sand the abandoned smooth beach-head;—
Maimed men, whose scars must be exhibited
To all the world, though much against your will—
And men whose bodies bear no marks of ill,
Being twisted only in the guts and head:
Come home! come home!—not to the home you long
To find,—and which your valour had achieved
Had virtue been but right, and evil wrong!—
We have tried hard, and we have greatly grieved:
Come home and help us!—you are hurt but strong!
—And we—we are bewildered—and bereaved.

Υ

Read history: so learn your place in Time;

And go to sleep: all this was done before;

We do it better, fouling every shore;

We disinfect, we do not probe, the crime.

Our engines plunge into the seas, they climb

Above our atmosphere: we grow not more

Profound as we approach the ocean's floor;

Our flight is lofty, it is not sublime.

Yet long ago this Earth by struggling men

Was scuffed, was scraped by mouths that bubbled mud;

And will be so again, and yet again;

Until we trace our poison to its bud

And root, and there uproot it: until then,

Earth will be warmed each winter by man's blood.

Υ

Read history: thus learn how small a space

You may inhabit, nor inhabit long

In crowding Cosmos—in that confined place

Work boldly; build your flimsy barriers strong;

Turn round and round, make warm your nest; among

The other hunting beasts, keep heart and face,—

Not to betray the doomed and splendid race

You are so proud of, to which you belong.

For trouble comes to all of us: the rat

Has courage, in adversity, to fight;

But what a shining animal is man,

Who knows, when pain subsides, that is not that,

For worse than that must follow—yet can write

Music; can laugh; play tennis; even plan.

Y

My words that once were virtuous and expressed
Nearly enough the mortal joys I knew,
Now that I sit to supper with the blest
Come haltingly, are very poor and few.
Whereof you speak and wherefore the bright walls
Resound with silver mirth I am aware,
But I am faint beneath the coronals
Of living vines you set upon my hair.
Angelic friends that stand with pointed wings
Sweetly demanding, in what dulcet tone,
How fare I in this heaven of happy things, —
I cannot lift my words against your own.
Forgive the downcast look, the lyre unstrung;
Breathing your presence, I forget your tongue.

Υ

Now sits the autumn cricket in the grass,
And on the gravel crawls the chilly bee;
Near to its close and none too soon for me
Draws the dull year, in which has come to pass
The changing of the happy child I was
Into this quiet creature people see
Stitching a seam with careful industry
To deaden you, who died on Michaelmas.
Ages ago the purple aconite
Laid its dark hoods about it on the ground,
And roses budded small and were content;
Swallows are south long since and out of sight;
With you the phlox and asters also went;
Nor can my laughter anywhere be found.

Υ

And must I then, indeed, Pain, live with you
All through my life?—sharing my fire, my bed,
Sharing—oh, worst of all things!—the same head?—
And, when I feed myself, feeding you, too?
So be it, then, if what seems true, is true:
Let us to dinner, comrade, and be fed;—
I cannot die till you yourself are dead,
And, with you living, I can live life through.
Yet have you done me harm, ungracious guest,
Spying upon my ardent offices
With frosty look; robbing my nights of rest;
And making harder things I did with ease.
You will die with me: but I shall, at best,
Forgive you with restraint, for deeds like these.

Υ

Grief that is grief and properly so hight
Has lodging in the orphaned brain alone,
Whose nest is cold, whose wings are now his own
And thinly feathered for the perchless flight
Between the owl and ermine; overnight
His food is reason, fodder for the grown,
His range is north to famine, south to fright.
When Constant Care was manna to the beak,
And Love Triumphant downed the hovering breast,
Vainly the cuckoo's child might nudge and speak
In ugly whispers to the indignant nest:
How even a feathered heart had power to break,
And thud no more above their huddled rest.

Υ

Felicity of Grief!—even Death being kind,
Reminding us how much we dared to love!
There, once, the challenge lay,—like a light glove
Dropped as through carelessness—easy to find
Means and excuse for being somewhat blind
Just at that moment; and why bend above,
Take up, such certain anguish for the mind?
Ah, you who suffer now as I now do,
Seeing, of Life's dimensions, not one left
Save Time—long days somehow to be lived through:
Think—of how great a thing were you bereft
That it should weigh so now!—and that you knew
Always, its awkward contours, and its heft.

Υ

If I die solvent—die, that is to say,
In full possession of my critical mind,
Not having cast, to keep the wolves at bay
In this dark wood—till all be flung behind—
Wit, courage, honour, pride, oblivion
Of the red eyeball and the yellow tooth;
Nor sweat nor howl nor break into a run
When loping Death's upon me in hot sooth;
'Twill be that in my honoured hands I bear
What's under no condition to be spilled
Till my blood spills and hardens in the air:
An earthen grail, a humble vessel filled
To its low brim with water from that brink
Where Shakespeare, Keats and Chaucer learned
        to drink.

Υ

What rider spurs him from the darkening east
As from a forest, and with rapid pound
Of hooves, now light, now louder on hard ground,
Approaches, and rides past with speed increased,
Dark spots and flecks of foam upon his beast?
What shouts he from the saddle, turning 'round,
As he rides on?—"Greetings!"—I made the sound;
"Greetings from Nineveh!"—it seemed, at least.

Did someone catch the object that he flung?
He held some object on his saddle-bow,
And flung it towards us as he passed; among
The children then it fell most likely; no,
'Tis here: a little bell without a tongue.
Listen; it has a faint voice even so.

Epitaph for the Race of Man

I

Before this cooling planet shall be cold,
Long, long before the music of the Lyre,
Like the faint roar of distant breakers rolled
On reefs unseen, when wind and flood conspire
To drive the ship inshore—long, long, I say,
Before this ominous humming hits the ear,
Earth will have come upon a stiller day,
Man and his engines be no longer here.
High on his naked rock the mountain sheep
Will stand alone against the final sky,
Drinking a wind of danger new and deep,
Staring on Vega with a piercing eye,
And gather up his slender hooves and leap
From crag to crag down Chaos, and so go by.

II

When Death was young and bleaching bones were few,

A moving hill against the risen day

The dinosaur at morning made his way,

And dropped his dung upon the blazing dew;

Trees with no name that now are agate grew

Lushly beside him in the steamy clay;

He woke and hungered, rose and stalked his prey,

And slept contented, in a world he knew.

In punctual season, with the race in mind,

His consort held aside her heavy tail,

And took the seed; and heard the seed confined

Roar in her womb; and made a nest to hold

A hatched-out conqueror . . . but to no avail:

The veined and fertile eggs are long since cold.

III

Cretaceous bird, your giant claw no lime
From bark of holly bruised or mistletoe
Could have arrested, could have held you so
Through fifty million years of jostling time;
Yet cradled with you in the catholic slime
Of the young ocean's tepid lapse and flow
Slumbered an agent, weak in embryo,
Should grip you straitly, in its sinewy prime.
What bright collision in the zodiac brews,
What mischief dimples at the planet's core
For shark, for python, for the dove that coos
Under the leaves?—what frosty fate's in store
For the warm blood of man,—man, out of ooze
But lately crawled, and climbing up the shore?

IV

O Earth, unhappy planet born to die,

Might I your scribe and your confessor be,

What wonders must you not relate to me

Of Man, who when his destiny was high

Strode like the sun into the middle sky

And shone an hour, and who so bright as he,

And like the sun went down into the sea,

Leaving no spark to be remembered by.

But no; you have not learned in all these years

To tell the leopard and the newt apart;

Man, with his singular laughter, his droll tears,

His engines and his conscience and his art,

Made but a simple sound upon your ears:

The patient beating of the animal heart.

V

When Man is gone and only gods remain
To stride the world, their mighty bodies hung
With golden shields, and golden curls outflung
Above their childish foreheads; when the plain
Round skull of Man is lifted and again
Abandoned by the ebbing wave, among
The sand and pebbles of the beach, — what tongue
Will tell the marvel of the human brain?
Heavy with music once this windy shell,
Heavy with knowledge of the clustered stars;
The one-time tenant of this draughty hall
Himself, in learned pamphlet, did foretell,
After some aeons of study jarred by wars,
This toothy gourd, this head emptied of all.

VI

See where Capella with her golden kids

Grazes the slope between the east and north:

Thus when the builders of the pyramids

Flung down their tools at nightfall and poured forth

Homeward to supper and a poor man's bed,

Shortening the road with friendly jest and slur,

The risen She-Goat showing blue and red

Climbed the clear dusk, and three stars followed her.

Safe in their linen and their spices lie

The kings of Egypt; even as long ago

Under these constellations, with long eye

And scented limbs they slept, and feared no foe.

Their will was law; their will was not to die:

And so they had their way; or nearly so.

VII

He heard the coughing tiger in the night
Push at his door; close by his quiet head
About the wattled cabin the soft tread
Of heavy feet he followed, and the slight
Sigh of the long banana leaves; in sight
At last and leaning westward overhead
The Centaur and the Cross now heralded
The sun, far off but marching, bringing light.

What time the Centaur and the Cross were spent,
Night and the beast retired into the hill,
Whereat serene and undevoured he lay,
And dozed and stretched and listened and lay still,
Breathing into his body with content
The temperate dawn before the tropic day.

VIII

Observe how Miyanoshita cracked in two
And slid into the valley; he that stood
Grinning with terror in the bamboo wood
Saw the earth heave and thrust its bowels through
The hill, and his own kitchen slide from view,
Spilling the warm bowl of his humble food
Into the lap of horror; mark how lewd
This cluttered gulf, —'twas here his paddy grew.

Dread and dismay have not encompassed him;
The calm sun sets; unhurried and aloof
Into the riven village falls the rain;
Days pass; the ashes cool; he builds again
His paper house upon oblivion's brim,
And plants the purple iris in its roof.

IX

He woke in terror to a sky more bright

Than middle day; he heard the sick earth groan,

And ran to see the lazy-smoking cone

Of the fire-mountain, friendly to his sight

As his wife's hand, gone strange and full of fright;

Over his fleeing shoulder it was shown

Rolling its pitchy lake of scalding stone

Upon his house that had no feet for flight.

Where did he weep? Where did he sit him down

And sorrow, with his head between his knees?

Where said the Race of Man, "Here let me drown"?

"Here let me die of hunger"?—"let me freeze"?

By nightfall he has built another town:

This boiling pot, this clearing in the trees.

X

The broken dike, the levee washed away,
The good fields flooded and the cattle drowned,
Estranged and treacherous all the faithful ground,
And nothing left but floating disarray
Of tree and home uprooted, — was this the day
Man dropped upon his shadow without a sound
And died, having laboured well and having found
His burden heavier than a quilt of clay?
No, no. I saw him when the sun had set
In water, leaning on his single oar
Above his garden faintly glimmering yet . . .
There bulked the plough, here washed the updrifted
        weeds . . .
And scull across his roof and make for shore,
With twisted face and pocket full of seeds.

XI

Sweeter was loss than silver coins to spend,

Sweeter was famine than the belly filled;

Better than blood in the vein was the blood spilled;

Better than corn and healthy flocks to tend

And a tight roof and acres without end

Was the barn burned and the mild creatures killed,

And the back aging fast, and all to build:

For then it was, his neighbour was his friend.

Then for a moment the averted eye

Was turned upon him with benignant beam,

Defiance faltered, and derision slept;

He saw as in a not unhappy dream

The kindly heads against the horrid sky,

And scowled, and cleared his throat and spat, and

wept.

XII

Now forth to meadow as the farmer goes
With shining buckets to the milking-ground,
He meets the black ant hurrying from his mound
To milk the aphis pastured on the rose;
But no good-morrow, as you might suppose,
No nod of greeting, no perfunctory sound
Passes between them; no occasion's found
For gossip as to how the fodder grows.
In chilly autumn on the hardening road
They meet again, driving their flocks to stall,
Two herdsmen, each with winter for a goad;
They meet and pass, and never a word at all
Gives one to t'other. On the quaint abode
Of each, the evening and the first snow fall.

XIII

His heatless room the watcher of the stars
Nightly inhabits when the night is clear;
Propping his mattress on the turning sphere,
Saturn his rings or Jupiter his bars
He follows, or the fleeing moons of Mars,
Till from his ticking lens they disappear. . . .
Whereat he sighs, and yawns, and on his ear
The busy chirp of Earth remotely jars.
Peace at the void's heart through the wordless night,
A lamb cropping the awful grasses, grazed;
Earthward the trouble lies, where strikes his light
At dawn industrious Man, and unamazed
Goes forth to plough, flinging a ribald stone
At all endeavour alien to his own.

XIV

Him not the golden fang of furious heaven,

Nor whirling Aeolus on his awful wheel,

Nor foggy spectre ramming the swift keel,

Nor flood, nor earthquake, nor the red tongue even

Of fire, disaster's dog—him, him bereaven

Of all save the heart's knocking, and to feel

The air upon his face: not the great heel

Of headless Force into the dust has driven.

These sunken cities, tier on tier, bespeak

How ever from the ashes with proud beak

And shining feathers did the phoenix rise,

And sail, and send the vulture from the skies . . .

That in the end returned; for Man was weak

Before the unkindness in his brother's eyes.

XV

Now sets his foot upon the eastern sill

Aldebaran, swiftly rising, mounting high,

And tracks the Pleiads down the crowded sky,

And drives his wedge into the western hill;

Now for the void sets forth, and further still,

The questioning mind of Man . . . that by and by

From the void's rim returns with swooning eye,

Having seen himself into the maelstrom spill.

O race of Adam, blench not lest you find

In the sun's bubbling bowl anonymous death,

Or lost in whistling space without a mind

To monstrous Nothing yield your little breath:

You shall achieve destruction where you stand,

In intimate conflict, at your brother's hand.

XVI

Alas for Man, so stealthily betrayed,
Bearing the bad cell in him from the start,
Pumping and feeding from his healthy heart
That wild disorder never to be stayed
When once established, destined to invade
With angry hordes the true and proper part,
Till Reason joggles in the headsman's cart,
And Mania spits from every balustrade.
Would he had searched his closet for his bane,
Where lurked the trusted ancient of his soul,
Obsequious Greed, and seen that visage plain;
Would he had whittled treason from his side
In his stout youth and bled his body whole,
Then had he died a king, or never died.

XVII

Only the diamond and the diamond's dust

Can render up the diamond unto Man;

One and invulnerable as it began

Had it endured, but for the treacherous thrust

That laid its hard heart open, as it must,

And ground it down and fitted it to span

A turbaned brow or fret an ivory fan,

Lopped of its stature, pared of its proper crust.

So Man, by all the wheels of heaven unscored,

Man, the stout ego, the exuberant mind

No edge could cleave, no acid could consume, —

Being split along the vein by his own kind,

Gives over, rolls upon the palm abhorred,

Is set in brass on the swart thumb of Doom.

XVIII

Here lies, and none to mourn him but the sea,

That falls incessant on the empty shore,

Most various Man, cut down to spring no more;

Before his prime, even in his infancy

Cut down, and all the clamour that was he,

Silenced; and all the riveted pride he wore,

A rusted iron column whose tall core

The rains have tunnelled like an aspen tree.

Man, doughty Man, what power has brought you low,

That heaven itself in arms could not persuade

To lay aside the lever and the spade

And be as dust among the dusts that blow?

Whence, whence the broadside? whose the heavy

   blade? . . .

Strive not to speak, poor scattered mouth; I know.

Finis

INDEX OF FIRST LINES

Heart, have no pity on this house of bone, 98
Here is a wound that never will heal, I know, 32
Here lies, and none to mourn him but the sea, 181
Him not the golden fang of furious heaven, 177
His heatless room the watcher of the stars, 176
His stalk the dark delphinium, 138
How healthily their feet upon the floor, 44
How innocent of me and my dark pain, 143

I, being born a woman and distressed, 41
I do but ask that you be always fair, 7
I dreamed I moved among the Elysian fields, 85
I know I am but summer to your heart, 27
I know my mind and I have made my choice, 114
I know the face of Falsehood and her tongue, 92
I must not die of pity; I must live, 142
I pray you if you love me, bear my joy, 28
I said in the beginning, did I not?, 110
I said, seeing how the winter gale increased, 82
I see so clearly now my similar years, 36
I shall forget you presently, my dear, 11

I shall go back again to the bleak shore, 33
I think I should have loved you presently, 9
I too beneath your moon, almighty Sex, 125
I will put Chaos into fourteen lines, 153
If I die solvent—die, that is to say, 162
If I should learn, in some quite casual way, 5
If in the years to come you should recall, 120
If there were balm in Gilead, I would go, 135
If to be left were to be left alone, 113
Into the golden vessel of great song, 13
It came into her mind, seeing how the snow, 56
It is the fashion now to wave aside, 150

Let you not say of me when I am old, 20
Life, were thy pains as are the pains of hell, 63
Lord Archer, Death, whom sent you in your stead?, 39
Love is not all: it is not meat nor drink, 99
Love is not blind. I see with single eye, 26
Love me no more, now let the god depart, 108
Love, though for this you riddle me with darts, 8
Loving you less than life, a little less, 40

Thou art not lovelier than
   lilacs,—no, *1*
Thou famished grave, I will not
   fill thee yet, *128*
Time does not bring relief; you
   all have lied, *2*
Time, that is pleased to lengthen
   out the day, *101*
Time, that renews the tissues of
   this frame, *124*
To hold secure the province of
   Pure Art, *148*
Tranquility at length, when
   autumn comes, *146*

Upon this age, that never speaks
   its mind, *140*
Upon this marble bust that is not
   I, *67*

We talk of taxes, and I call you
   friend, *12*
Well, I have lost you; and I lost
   you fairly, *116*
What chores these churls do put
   upon the great, *152*
What lips my lips have kissed,
   and where, and why, *42*
What rider spurs him from the
   darkening east, *163*
What thing is this that, built of
   salt and lime, *70*

What's this of death, from you
   who never will die?, *35*
When Death was young and
   bleaching bones were few, *165*
When did I ever deny, though
   this was fleeting, *127*
When I too long have looked
   upon your face, *18*
When Man is gone and only gods
   remain, *168*
When we are old and these
   rejoicing veins, *97*
When we that wore the myrtle
   wear the dust, *100*
When you are dead, and your
   disturbing eyes, *78*
When you, that at this moment
   are to me, *24*
Where can the heart be hidden in
   the ground, *123*
Whereas at morning in a jeweled
   crown, *93*
Women have loved before as I
   love now, *95*

Yet in an hour to come,
   disdainful dust, *77*
You loved me not at all, but let it
   go, *109*
You say: "Since life is cruel
   enough at best," *107*
Your face is like a chamber where
   a king, *37*